From an etching by E. P. Metour, by permission of E. H. Curlander, Art Dealer, Baltimore

THE STATE HOUSE FROM CHANCERY LANE

To

THE "PEGGY STEWART" TEA PARTY CHAPTER

D. A. R.

ANNAPOLIS
— MARYLAND —

Its Colonial and Naval Story

with
Selections from Diaries
and Private Letters

Illustrated with
Etchings by Eugene P. Metour
and
Drawings by Vernon Howe Bailey

Walter B. Norris

HERITAGE BOOKS
2008

HERITAGE BOOKS
AN IMPRINT OF HERITAGE BOOKS, INC.

Books, CDs, and more—Worldwide

For our listing of thousands of titles see our website
at
www.HeritageBooks.com

A Facsimile Reprint
Published 2008 by
HERITAGE BOOKS, INC.
Publishing Division
100 Railroad Ave. #104
Westminster, Maryland 21157

Copyright © 1925 Thomas Y. Crowell Company

— Publisher's Notice —
In reprints such as this, it is often not possible to remove blemishes from the original. In addition, the illustrations listed for page 38a are missing. We feel the contents of this book warrant its reissue despite these blemishes and hope you will agree and read it with pleasure.

International Standard Book Numbers
Paperbound: 978-1-55613-223-0
Clothbound: 978-0-7884-7726-3

FOREWORD

In his "Richard Carvel" Winston Churchill paints a charming picture of the society of Annapolis in the days just before the Revolution. The figures are largely fictitious, the setting a novelist's adaptation of history, but the whole a truthful portrayal of the life of the time. The authentic story of the town has, however, never been told briefly and comprehensively enough to secure the attention of the average American, and this fact is the justification for the present volume. In it an effort has been made to picture especially the homes of Colonial Annapolis, the family histories of the principal inhabitants, the life of the clubs, theaters, and coffee houses, the controversies that dot the pages of the *Maryland Gazette,* the manifestations of activity in literature and art, and the dignified patriotism of the Revolutionary struggle.

He who writes the history of Annapolis finds himself drawn in two different directions. One is the delightful aspects of Colonial society just mentioned, the other the history and life of the United States Navy as developed in the institution for the training of its officers which has here always had its home. Both deserve fuller treatment than they receive, and the proportion of space devoted to each can be justified only by the interest of the reader, but the author regrets that more of the material available on each could not be included.

In the story of any town traditions have an honored place, and the present writer makes no apology for including, as traditions, statements for which no direct proof is discoverable. But in giving history, not hearsay, he has endeavored to qualify all statements which are not verifiable. Even if Annapolis may therefore not claim that its original State House was the product of the brain of Sir Christopher Wren, or that its theater was the first in America, it still possesses adequate attractions for any one to whom the past is more than an outworn garment to be discarded and forgotten.

In the preparation of the material here presented, the author is under obligations to many persons, not all of whom are named in the bibliographical footnotes. To the staffs of the Maryland State Library and the Library of the United States Naval Academy his debt has been constant and their patience great. The librarians of the Maryland Historical Society, the Peabody Library, Baltimore, and the Division of Manuscripts of the Library of Congress have also been generous with their interest and assistance.

The chief unacknowledged debt is to Scharf's "History of Maryland," a monument of painstaking scholarship; to David Ridgley's "Annals of Annapolis" and to Elihu Riley's "The Ancient City," that rich compendium of extracts from the *Maryland Gazette* and of its author's inexhaustible memory, recourse has been had on many an occasion.

For the illustrations which do so much to convey to the reader the architectural and other artistic charms of the town, I am under special obligation to Professor Eugene P. Metour, of Williams College, for the privilege of reproducing some of the etchings he executed while a resident of Annapolis. Without these, and the drawings by Mr. Vernon Howe Bailey here reproduced by permission of *Harper's Magazine,* the appeal of Annapolis to the artist could not be adequately portrayed. I am also indebted to Mr. Louis Ruyl, of New York, and to the *Lucky Bag* of the Class of 1922, U.S. N.A., for permission to use illustrations which it was later found impossible to include. In the same way I wish to express appreciation for similar courtesies from Mr. E. S. Olmsted, of Des Moines, Iowa, father of the late Jerauld L. Olmsted, editor-in-chief of the *Lucky Bag* above mentioned.

TABLE OF CONTENTS

CHAPTER		PAGE
I.	A City of Historic Charm	1
II.	A Puritan Settlement in a Catholic Colony	10
III.	The Revolution of 1688 Makes Annapolis the Provincial Capital .	26
IV.	A City of Wealth and Fashion . .	42
V.	Clubs, Theaters and Literature .	61
VI.	Some Tory Families and Their Homes	92
VII.	The Three Signers of the Declaration of Independence and Their Annapolis Homes	109
VIII.	A Glance at Annapolis Before the Revolution	125
IX.	Stamp Act Riots and the "Peggy Stewart" Tea Party	136
X.	Opening the Revolution—a Contest in Courtesy	154
XI.	Lafayette and Rochambeau in Annapolis, 1781	177
XII.	Washington Visits Annapolis . .	191
XIII.	In Genteel Eclipse	225

CHAPTER		PAGE
XIV.	FORT SEVERN BECOMES THE NAVAL ACADEMY	245
XV.	THE CIVIL WAR AND "BEN" BUTLER REACH ANNAPOLIS	263
XVI.	SINCE THE CIVIL WAR	276
APPENDIX I		293
APPENDIX II		293
APPENDIX III		298
INDEX		301

ILLUSTRATIONS

STATE HOUSE FROM CHANCERY LANE....*Frontispiece*
From an etching by E. P. Metour

                                                          FACING PAGE

THE BRICE HOUSE, BUILT ABOUT 1745....... 6
From a drawing by Vernon Howe Bailey

THE PACA HOUSE, NOW CARVEL HALL HOTEL, BUILT ABOUT 1763 20
From a drawing by Vernon Howe Bailey

MARKET SLIP 38
From an etching by E. P. Metour

DILAPIDATED DOCKS 56
From an etching by E. P. Metour

THE DR. JOHN SHAW HOUSE, NOW THE ELKS' CLUB, AND STATE CIRCLE 74
From a drawing by Vernon Howe Bailey

THE CARROLL HOUSE, NOW ST. MARY'S RECTORY, BUILT ABOUT 1735 112
From a drawing by Vernon Howe Bailey

THE CHASE HOUSE, BUILT ABOUT 1770 120
From a photograph by Pickering, Annapolis

THE STATE HOUSE FROM NORTH STREET......... 148
From an etching by E. P. Metour

DRYING SAILS IN MARKET SLIP 166
From an etching by E. P. Metour

Illustrations

	FACING PAGE
THE OLD SENATE CHAMBER	194

From a photograph by Pickering, Annapolis

WASHINGTON, LAFAYETTE AND TENCH TILGHMAN ... 218
  From the portrait by Charles Willson Peale in the Old Senate Chamber; photograph by Pickering, Annapolis

DOCK STREET AND MARKET ... 240
  From an etching by E. P. Metour

IN NEED OF REPAIRS ... 254
  From an etching by E. P. Metour

MAHAN HALL, NAVAL ACADEMY ... 282
  From a photograph by Pickering, Annapolis

THE NAVAL ACADEMY CHAPEL ... 288
  From a photograph by Pickering, Annapolis

ANNAPOLIS: ITS COLONIAL AND NAVAL STORY

CHAPTER I

A CITY OF HISTORIC CHARM

ANNAPOLIS, the ancient capital of Maryland, with its century-old State House lifting its slender wooden dome as delicate as Chippendale above its highest hill, is a town with a charm all its own. Not because it contains houses and survivals of Colonial times but because with all these it has retained something of the very atmosphere of the rollicking days before the Revolution. As it has never expanded commercially it has never changed its character and has preserved its old buildings, streets, alleys, and general air of cultivated, aristocratic complacency. The coming of the Naval Academy in the middle of the last century did not destroy Colonial Annapolis but merely enabled it to achieve sufficient material prosperity to maintain its gentility.

Blue water, red brick, and green shade, with the white dome of the State House above them all, just about express one's impression of Annapolis in the pleasant months of the year, which here stretch from March to December. Almost surrounded by the blue Severn and its tributary inlets, Annapolis is essentially a maritime community with rakish Chesapeake Bay oyster schooners lying at anchor before the town, not to speak of the presence of the Naval Academy with its fleet of cutters manned by white-clothed midshipmen, darting submarine chasers, and an occasional cruiser and grim battleship lying out in the Roads. And wherever one turns, his farthest glance down the street is likely to rest upon a bit of blue water or the slope of a mast and sail.

But the real charm of the town is in its fragrant past. Its streets are narrow, like Boston's, but unlike them rarely need to be wider. They are generally straight, except where they describe circles around the State House and St. Anne's ancient churchyard to confuse and lose the wandering visitor. From these circles the streets lead out like spokes from the hub of

A City of Historic Charm

a wheel. Their very names cast ghostly shadows of an aristocratic past: Duke of Gloucester, Queen Anne's only child who survived infancy; King George; Prince George, the name of Anne's almost forgotten husband; Hanover; Cornhill; Fleet—some of its founders evidently loved London—Dean; Cathedral—this was to have been a cathedral town; Charles,—all have remained without change since from before the Revolution.

Even the alleys are a delight and a novelty to one who has not traversed the older parts of London. They cut across from street to street in a surprising but helpful way, and Chancery Lane and Carroll Alley have a past as rich as any avenue. Like the city ordinances that till recently authorized the appointment of an inspector of chimney sweeps and established regulations for the proper sweeping of chimneys, they bring back a past that is too delightful to be obliterated.

Even if familiarity makes one forget the thrill of street names, one never loses pleasure in the beautiful Colonial residences that dot the town. In the midst of many modern dwellings, hardly a street fails to boast one or more charming relics of Georgian architecture at its best. Coming out of a narrow alley, one glances up the street to feast one's eyes on the majestic outlines of such a mansion as the Brice House, of old brick, with classic cornice and hall window, and great end chimneys. At each side is the low-roofed wing overgrown with ivy that was originally the servants' quarters or kitchen or domestic offices. Inside, the high ceilings, ancient wainscoting, and stately fireplaces, all make one feel that he has stepped into a larger, more lordly time. And happy will he be to secure lodging, as he may, even in what was the kitchen or servant's bedroom, for these do not lack the simple beauty of Georgian building and decoration.

With such houses to delight the eye, viewpoints come to be cherished, and one goes a longer way that he may see again some gem of architecture from a point he has found especially fine. As he gazes and walks the scenes of "Richard Carvel" seem as if of yesterday, and he almost expects to see Dorothy Manners or Captain Clapsaddle appear before him and go off, she in a sedan chair and he on his sturdy saddle horse.

A City of Historic Charm

Even in the negro quarter one occasionally discovers an old house which still stands in real beauty amid the squatty tenements.

Above all the houses and forming the cynosure of the town and vicinity is the lofty dome of the State House. It sits easily based on the ancient part of the capitol, rising in slender outline white against the sky, and so light and graceful that the eye is fascinated. From all parts of the town the streets lead toward it and thus afford many a varied picture of its charms.

As one enters the portals of these historic structures, public or private, one meets the old-fashioned courtesy and gentility which is one of the permanent remains of the South before the Civil War. And one finds a social grace in men and women which shows itself in a simple but sincere hospitality which has always been noted by visitors to Annapolis and which is one of the best inheritances from previous generations.

In the unbustling atmosphere of the town, calling is a social custom that still persists, fostered partly by the official requirements of the naval service but also by strength of ancient custom. An American Mrs. Gaskell would find no better setting for her characters than here, where a lady has an "afternoon at home" and during at least the winter months devotes some time nearly every afternoon to eating the sandwiches and drinking the tea provided by successive hostesses of her acquaintance. Here exists in an inexplicable fashion—until one remembers that Annapolis has always been Southern and that the spirit of the Southern plantation owner was a Colonial spirit and that the South never really changes—the air of unconcern with the serious things of life which reminds one of the days of Steele and Addison and which is reflected so brilliantly in the many sprightly and lovely private letters that Annapolitan *chatelaines* of the past have left us.

The naval atmosphere which at present dominates the life and thought of Annapolis does not really obliterate the chief qualities of the earlier period. In its emphasis on formality and its generally aristocratic tone the Navy fits perfectly into the picture of the past. Social forms and the usual features of higher society, the call, the ball, and the dinner party, are still found, even though the naval officer, as well as the

*From a drawing by Vernon Howe Bailey
by permission of Harpers Magazine*

THE BRICE HOUSE

A City of Historic Charm

present day Annapolitan, supports these on an income which would hardly have supplied Richard Carvel with his claret. And there is also a constant memory of traditions of the naval profession as evidenced by the many memorials and mementos of famous men and events that dot the Academy grounds. In Bancroft Hall, high on the wall where no midshipman can fail to notice it, is spread the flag which has given the Navy its watchword, Lawrence's dying words on the *Chesapeake* inscribed on the rude piece of blue which Perry flew at Lake Erie spelling out "Don't Give Up the Ship." And from *Guerrière, Macedonian, Java, Lady Prevost,* and other captured frigates and sloops of the second war of independence have come trophies that bring us directly in touch with the earlier times. And in his imperial marble sarcophagus in the crypt of the Academy chapel sleeps Paul Jones, who, as every reader of Churchill's stirring story of the town knows, prized every fashionable appurtenance of his time.

Few towns in America have thus a more varied store of historical interest than the little capital by the Severn. Like Bruges and Perugia, Warwick and Nuremberg, its charm lies in its actual preservation of the atmosphere of the past in everything except flesh and blood, not mere sites where famous actions took place but the very houses, streets, and drawing rooms in all their original character. Here is no museum or museum-like atmosphere, but the town itself is a living museum with everything in a natural setting.

It ought, therefore, to be worth the while of every American who venerates the historic foundations of the nation to-day, and the men who laid those foundations so well, to trace the growth of one town where these facts are so evident. In its varied history he will see its Puritan origin in a Catholic colony, its fortunes changing with the rise and fall of party in the mother country, its rapid strides to affluence and luxury from the profits of the tobacco field, its sturdy assertion of the rights of freemen against Parliamentary oppression, its burning of the hated tea in emulation of Boston's example, its support of the cause of the Colonies in its firm but dignified fashion, its sympathetic reception of the aristocratic French officers fresh from the court of Louis XVI, its social intimacies with Colonel, and then later, General Washington, its preservation from decay by the establishment of the Naval Academy, its "capture" in 1861 by the redoubtable "Ben" Butler, and its refining influences upon all the principal naval characters who emerged from their midshipman days to prove their sterling qualities as junior officers in the war between the States, whether they were under the Stars or the Bars, as commanding officers at Manila and Santiago, and in both capacities in the world-wide activities of the defeat of Germany. Such a survey will present an almost perfect cross-section of American achievement in war and peace, in commerce, education, politics, and the more elegant phases of social life.

CHAPTER II

A PURITAN SETTLEMENT IN A CATHOLIC COLONY

THE origin of Annapolis as a settlement is interestingly bound up with the interplay of Royalist and Roundhead politics in England and with the delicate position in which Lord Baltimore, the Royalist and Catholic friend and supporter of Charles I, was placed by his politics and his religion when Parliament espoused the cause of the Puritans in the fifth decade of the seventeenth century. The founding of Annapolis was perhaps chiefly due to Lord Baltimore's efforts to save his colony of Maryland from being taken away from him because of his loyalty to Charles I.

Already in 1634 Leonard Calvert, his brother, had established the colony on a branch of the Potomac at St. Mary's in southern Maryland, but the settlement had not prospered. Upon the execution of Charles I in 1649, Lord Balti-

A Puritan Settlement 11

more renewed his efforts to secure settlers, and especially Protestants. Although in the very beginning of the colony Lord Baltimore had proclaimed religious freedom—he could do little else if he wished the Catholics protected—in 1649 he caused the Assembly of the colony to pass the famous Toleration Act, which read:

"No person or persons whatsoever within this province or the islands, ports, harbors, creeks, or havens thereunto belonging, professing to believe in Jesus Christ, shall from henceforth be anyways troubled, molested, or discountenanced, for or in respect of his or her religion, nor in the free exercise thereof within this province or the islands thereunto belonging."

This not only assured Protestants that they would be welcome in the colony, but also strengthened the security of the Catholics already there, who much needed it when the Puritans came into power in the mother country.

Even before this, in 1648, Lord Baltimore had appointed a Protestant Governor, made three Protestants members of the Council of the colony, and appointed another Protestant the Provincial Secretary. William Stone, the new

Governor, was a Virginian who had apparently offered to bring with him into the Chesapeake country a large number of new settlers. These he found already in America, and not far away, in Virginia about what is now Norfolk. The group chiefly consisted of a number of Puritan families who had, in 1642, been brought over by Richard Bennett, nephew of one of the Governors of the Virginia Company. Members of an Independent church in England, they had emigrated to secure the same privileges in religious worship and community life that had sent the Scrooby Pilgrims to Plymouth only a few years before them. Even as early as 1638 Puritans had settled about Sewell's Point near where the Jamestown Exposition was later held.

But soon they found themselves persecuted even in the New World. The Virginia colony was Royalist and anxious that the supremacy of the Established Church should be maintained in Virginia as well as in England. Accordingly, several Puritan ministers whom Bennett had secured from Boston were expelled, some of the chief members of the settlement summoned to court for refusing to hear common

A Puritan Settlement 13

prayer, and the free exercise of Puritan ideas of worship generally interfered with.[1]

To these people William Stone offered an asylum in Maryland, even promising that the oath of fidelity to Lord Baltimore would be changed so that these Roundheads would not be obliged to swear allegiance to a Royalist and Catholic. Some had probably already come.

In 1648, William Durand, one of the leaders of the group, had come to the Severn to examine the opportunity offered, and in the two years that followed the whole body apparently migrated to Maryland and settled at the mouth of the Severn and along the shore of the Chesapeake down to the Patuxent. At the former place the town, called Providence, was laid out on the northern side at the very mouth of the river, near where Greenberry Point Light House now stands. Here considerable land has been gradually washed away by the action of the waves.

The triumphs of the Parliamentary party in England and the coming of Cromwell to power

[1] See D. R. Randall, "A Puritan Colony in Maryland," Johns Hopkins University Historical Studies, Fourth Series, No. 6.

soon inspired the Puritans with hopes for the triumph of their cause politically and religiously in Maryland. They at once became openly antagonistic to the government of the province. First, they refused to take the oath of fidelity in spite of the fact that this was required to gain title to the land which every settler was given for coming into the colony. In consequence much litigation later took place. But soon the expectations of the Puritans were fulfilled. In 1651 Parliament appointed commissioners to reduce and reorganize the Virginia colony, and although Lord Baltimore managed to have the word Maryland omitted from their instructions, enough was said about the lands on the Chesapeake to furnish a pretext for the two commissioners who actually undertook the enterprise to go ahead and interfere in the affairs of Maryland. For these two men were no other than the Richard Bennett who had brought the Severn settlers to Virginia, and William Claiborne, a Virginian who had clashed with Lord Baltimore several years before by establishing a trading post on Kent Island just opposite the mouth of the Severn and had refused to acknowledge the

A Puritan Settlement 15

authority of the Catholic Proprietary. He had been finally ejected only by the armed forces of Lord Baltimore in the first naval conflict in Maryland waters.

With such support it was not long before the Puritans controlled the colony. But Lord Baltimore's previous strategy in appointing a Protestant governor and bringing in Protestant settlers was not in vain, for Cromwell did not take the colony away from him, and Parliament by denying the petitions of the most extreme Puritans enabled him to assert in 1655 that his authority had been confirmed. He thereupon ordered Governor Stone to proclaim the fact and to require the Severn Puritans to acknowledge his sovereignty. At the head of 200 men with eleven boats to assist in crossing the rivers Stone marched from St. Mary's toward the Severn to bring the recalcitrant Puritans to terms. This led to the so-called Battle of the Severn in 1655, the first important event in the history of Annapolis.

The engagement took place on March 25th on the southern side of what is now Spa Creek, which stretches along the southern side of the town. Stone and his forces had sailed into the Severn, passed by the site of Annapolis, and landed on the lower side of the creek. The Puritans had assembled on the opposite side of the Severn, and had impressed a ship anchored in the river for the purpose of blockading Stone's forces in the creek. This ship, the *Golden Lion,* commanded by Roger Heamans, was also assisted by a small New England vessel armed with two guns. Meanwhile the Puritan forces crossed the river to a point from which they could swing around to the south and attack Lord Baltimore's men from the rear. In the rather sharp conflict which followed the Puritan commander, Captain Fuller, with his one hundred and twenty men completely routed the Proprietary's forces. Practically all of these were captured, including Stone himself. The number of killed and wounded on both sides was about fifty. Ten of the leaders of the defeated force were condemned to death but only four were actually shot. Stone was not among these.

The intensity of feeling on both sides is well shown by the numerous printed accounts and discussions of the affair that still exist. Heamans, the captain of the *Golden Lion,* published in London the year of the engagement "Narrative of a Late Bloody Design Against the Protestants of Anne Arundel County,"[1] in which he tells the story of the battle and charges that the chief men of the Catholic party tried to persuade a former seaman of the *Golden Lion* to fire on the ship and blow her up. His story runs:

"Suddenly or within two hours after at the most, in the very shutting up of the day's light, the ship's (*Golden Lion's*) company descried off a company of sloops and boats working toward the ship; whereupon the Council on board and the ship's company would have made shot at them, but the relator (Heamans) commanded them to forbear and went himself upon the poop on the stern of his ship and hailed them several times and no answer was made."

Finally fired on twice, the boats of Stone's force rowed off, "calling the ship's company rogues, Roundheads — rogues and dogs, and

[1] Printed in *Maryland Historical Magazine,* Vol. IV, p. 140 ff.

with many execrations and railings threatening to fire upon them in the morning."

Even more colorful is the account of the affair written to Lord Baltimore by the wife of Governor Stone while her husband was still a captive in the hands of the Puritans. She writes:

"I am sorry at present for to let your honor understand of our sad condition in your province. Sort is, that my husband with the rest of your Council went about a month agone with a party of men up to Anne Arundel County, to bring those factious people to obedience under your government. My husband sent Dr. Barber with one Mr. Coursey with a message to them, but they never returned again before the fight began. Also he sent over one Mr. Packer the day after, with a message, and he likewise never returned, as I heard: but so it was, that upon Sunday the 25th of March they did engage with the people of Anne Arundel, and lost the field, and not above five of our men escaped; which I did conceive ran away before the fight was ended; the rest all taken, some killed and wounded; my husband hath received a wound in his shoulder, but I hear it is upon the mending.

"My husband, I am confident, did not think that they would have engaged, but it did prove too true to all our great damages; they, as I hear, being better provided than my husband did expect; for they hired the captain of the *Golden Lion,* a great ship of burden, the captain's name is Roger Heamans, a young man, and his brother, who have been great sticklers in the business, as I hear. Captain Heamans was one of their council of war, and by his consent would have had all the prisoners hanged; but after quarter given, they tried all your Councillors by a council of war, and sentence was passed upon my husband to be shot to death, but was after saved by the enemy's own soldiers, and so the rest of the Councillors were saved by the petitions of the women, with some other friends which they found there; only Master William Eltonhead was shot to death, whose death I much lament, being shot in cold blood; and also Lieutenant William Lewis, with one Mr. Leggat and a German, which did live with Mr. Eltonhead, which by all relations that ever did hear of, the like barbarous act was never done amongst Christians.

"They have sequestered my husband's estate, only they say they will allow a maintenance for me and my children, which I do believe will be but small. They keep my husband, with the rest of the Council, and all other officers, still prisoners; I am very suddenly, God willing, bound up to see my husband. They will not so much as suffer him to write a letter unto me, but they will have the perusal of what he writes.

"Captain Tilghman and his mate Master Cook are very honest men, and do stand up much for your Honor; they will inform you of more passages than I can remember at the present; and I hope my brother will be down before Captain Tilghman goes away, and will write to you more at large; for he is bound up this day for to see his brother, if they do not detain him there as well as the rest; the occasion I conceive of their detainment there is, because they should not go home to inform your Honor of the truth of the business before they make their own tale in England, which let them do their worst, which I do not question

From a drawing by Vernon Howe Bailey
by permission of Harper's Magazine

THE PACA HOUSE, NOW CARVEL HALL HOTEL, BUILT BY WILLIAM PACA

but you will vindicate my husband's honor which hath ventured life and estate to keep your due here, which by force he hath lost.

"And they give out words that they have won the country by the sword, and by it they will keep the same, let my Lord Protector send in what writing he pleaseth. The Gunner's Mate of Heamans, since his coming down from Anne Arundel to Patuxent, hath boasted that he shot the first man that was shot of our party. All this I write is very true, which I thought good to inform your Lordship, because they will not suffer my husband for to write himself. I hope your Honor will be pleased for to look upon my son, and for to wish him for to be of good comfort, and not for to take our afflictions to heart.

And nothing else at present, I rest
Your Honor's most humble servant
VIRLINDA STONE.

"Post-Script: I hope your Honor will favor me so much that if my son wants twenty or thirty pounds you will let him have it, and it shall be paid your Honor again.

"Heamans, the master of the *Golden Lion*, is a very knave, and that will be made plainly for to appear to your Lordship, for he hath abused my husband most grossly." [1]

When Charles II came to the throne, the Puritans of the Severn quietly submitted to the rule of Lord Baltimore. This was largely due to his judicious methods of handling the situation, for he made no reprisals and admitted Protestants and rebels to the Governor's Council. The settlers of Providence thus lost none of the privileges which they had sought by their original migration from Virginia.

Already in 1650 the settlers had sent two burgesses to the provincial Assembly, and one of these had been elected Speaker. In 1650 Col. Edward Lloyd, Gentleman, one of their chief military men, had also been appointed commander of the armed forces of the Severn section, and he was later a member of the Governor's Council. To him is probably due the very name of the river, which like his name is obviously Welsh. Later when he moved to the

[1] "Refutation of 'Babylon's Fall,'" by John Langford, Gentleman, London, 1655.

A Puritan Settlement 23

Eastern Shore of Maryland he bestowed other Welsh names, Wye and Tred Avon, on rivers there.

In 1650 the section had also been made a county extending north and west almost indefinitely from the Severn. This had been named Anne Arundel in honor of the daughter of the Earl of Arundel, who became the wife of the second Lord Baltimore. The settlement on Greenberry Point, which had originally been known as Town Neck, was given the Puritan name of Providence. But this site never grew into a town, for the immigrants preferred to scatter about on plantations of considerable extent, and when traders and other townspeople came they preferred the present location of Annapolis. This was originally called Proctor's Landing from Richard Proctor, one of the earliest inhabitants. Later it was known as Anne Arundel Town or as either Severn or Proctor's until 1695, when it was formally named Annapolis in honor of Princess Anne, daughter of James II, but a Protestant, and later Queen.

Trading with the Indians was one of the

early activities of the settlers. Richard Bennett, who had originally secured the land on Greenberry Point, sold it to Nathaniel Utie, an extensive trader and a member of the Governor's Council in 1654. As in Virginia, however, the chief product was tobacco. The records also show that there was very frequent intercourse between the Chesapeake Bay settlers and the Dutch on the Delaware and the Hudson. Adventurers from these settlements moved to Maryland, and runaway servants from one to the other were not uncommon and caused frequent disputes.

One can therefore imagine the new settlement as scattered along the Severn and not concentrated on any one spot. Indians were common and often troublesome. The Susquehannocks, who had been pushed south by the Senecas so that they were chiefly found on the western shore of the Chesapeake as far south as the Severn, were a powerful and warlike tribe, much in contrast to the peaceful Piscataways who had welcomed Calvert to southern Maryland. With the Susquehannocks, however, the Puritans concluded a treaty in 1652 which al-

A Puritan Settlement 25

lowed the whites to settle around the head of Chesapeake and down both its shores, and this treaty seems to have prevented any serious trouble. Tradition testifies that it was concluded and signed under the huge tulip poplar tree that still stands on the campus of St. John's College.

CHAPTER III

THE REVOLUTION OF 1688 MAKES ANNAPOLIS THE PROVINCIAL CAPITAL

DURING the forty years following the victory of the Puritans on the Severn, the country about that river made rapid strides in settlement and soon became the chief of all the parts of the province. The colonists, however, did not tend to settle in towns, and in 1683 the Assembly passed an Act to encourage their development. Certain towns were established and given rights and special prestige. Although some of these never became populous, the town at Proctor's, or Anne Arundel Town, from this time on grew in official importance. It was made the residence of the district collector, the naval officer, and of the deputies for the dispatch of shipping. The Act provided that only from such legally established ports should ships clear with their cargoes of tobacco, and to them all ships from outside the colony must

Annapolis the Provincial Capital 27

come before discharging their goods and passengers.

The greatest impetus to its development that Annapolis received was, however, the events in England that resulted in deposing James II and setting on the throne the joint rulers, William of Orange, the Hollander, and Mary Stuart, the Protestant daughter of the Catholic James. Just as the execution of Charles I had indirectly resulted in bringing the Puritans to the Severn, so the fate of James II led to the establishment of a new party in Maryland and the removal of the capital from St. Mary's, Catholic and friendly to Lord Baltimore, to Annapolis, strongly in sympathy with Parliament and Protestantism. Its honor of being the capital Annapolis has ever since tenaciously retained, though in the last hundred years Baltimore has become the real center of commercial and political activity.

As early as 1674 we find the people of the town offering it as the site for a new capital, and promising to provide a State House, a prison, offices, and even a suitable house for the Governor—all to be paid for by the province when they had been finished. But it was not till the Revolution of 1688 that they had their opportunity.

By that time enough friction had arisen between the Proprietor and the Assembly for the religious issue to dominate the situation. The Protestants were in the majority in the colony, with their chief strength at the Severn; the principal officials, however, were appointed by the Proprietor and were naturally Catholic and antagonistic to the Assembly and its insistence upon popular government. In the thought of most of the settlers, James II and Lord Baltimore were linked as Catholics and tyrants, and the coming to the throne of a sovereign placed there by Parliament and a wave of Protestant feeling must mean, they felt, that a corresponding change should take place in the colony.

As, moreover, William of Orange was naturally anxious to strengthen his hold upon the government of the country and its colonies, for his crown was threatened by followers of James in every part of his domains, it was not difficult to secure his assistance. There were, of course, abuses in Lord Baltimore's administration, but these never seem to have been proved; rather what may justly be called a revolutionary movement took place which seized the control of the affairs of the colony under color of a grave danger of Indian attack—an attack which existed only in the imaginations of the agitators—and which found William so anxious for support that he was willing to abet them in their illegal methods for the benefits he would obtain.

Curiously enough, the people of Anne Arundel were not the leaders in this revolutionary proceeding, for they seem to have held aloof and allowed persons in the southern counties, where religious feeling was kept alive by the presence of many Catholics, to lead. The result was, however, that the so-called Associators led by a clergyman of the Established Church, John Coode, overturned the government of Lord Baltimore and offered the colony to King William. After slight and never conclusive investigation into the charges against Lord Baltimore, William appointed a royal Governor, Sir Lionel Copley, and Maryland became a royal province.

Three years later, in 1694, when Sir Lionel was succeeded by Sir Francis Nicholson, the latter called the Assembly to meet, not at St. Mary's but at Anne Arundel Town. The reasons were probably chiefly political in that it removed the members from the atmosphere of the section where Lord Baltimore was more favorably regarded and where William's action was not so popular. But a better reason was the geographical advantages of the new capital. Situated about half way up the Chesapeake, which separated the Eastern Shore and the Western Shore, as they were officially called, but which in a truer sense afforded easy means of communication between the various parts of the colony, it had a central location which justified its choice in days when travel by land was difficult and the rivers and bays the most natural routes.

The chief citizen of the town at this period would seem to have been Major Edward Dorsey. In his brick mansion—still standing on Prince George Street—the first session of the Assembly was held in February, 1695. It is recorded that at one time they gave great offense to the Governor by adjourning to an alehouse nearby, but in other respects they seem to have loyally assisted him in his efforts to make the town a worthy capital for the colony. A ferry was set up for crossing the Severn, a handsome pair of gates was erected at the town's western entrance, and two triangular sentry boxes constructed for the rangers who were to guard the gates.

In laying out the new capital modern principles of zoning and city planning were utilized. The section on the highest elevation was reserved for public buildings—the present site of the State House—and the land from there to the Severn was for the mansions of the gentlemen of the community. Trade was to be conducted largely to the west and south of these sections, and industries such as tanning, baking, brewing, and dyeing were assigned spots where the sights and odors would not be objectionable to the citizens.

Governor Nicholson was in many respects the real founder of the city. One of the buildings he erected still stands,—the small brick structure on the State House grounds built in the shape of a Greek cross and usually called the Old Treasury Building. It was built in his time but the exact date is unknown. First used primarily as a place for the meetings of the Governor's Council, it has served all sorts of uses. During periods when the State House could not be occupied it has served for the Assembly and probably housed the Annapolis Convention which led directly to the Constitutional Convention in Philadelphia which framed the Constitution of the United States.

The Governor also pushed ahead work on a brick State House, which was completed in 1697. When this was consumed by fire in 1704, another was erected on the same site and stood till the present building replaced it in 1772. For many years it was also used as the county court house, and is often so called. On a large plot of land lying between the State House and the harbor Governor Nicholson erected a house for himself with garden, vineyard, and summer house. It stood till about 1870, a wooden structure of one story and a half with a hip roof.

Governor Nicholson was also very much interested in founding a school, for there seems to have been none in the colony, although the few clergymen who had settled there often eked out their meager incomes by teaching boys. Now he proposed a free school furnished with a "school master, usher, and a writing master that can cast accounts," and he started the subscription toward defraying the necessary expenses. Members of the Council and the Assembly contributed various sums from 5,000 pounds of tobacco to one gold guinea, and a brick school building was completed in 1701 on a plot of ground situated just south of the State House and presented by the Governor. Its location is suggested by the name of School Street to-day. In the building lived the school teacher and his family.

Education was placed on an even stronger foundation by an Act of the Assembly in the same year as the subscription just mentioned, 1694, by which money for the maintenance of schools was to be derived from taxes imposed on furs, beef, bacon, and exports from the province. To the school in Annapolis, which largely profited from these revenues, was given the name of King William's School, and trustees were to be appointed by the King and the Governor. The Chancellor was to be the Archbishop of Canterbury.

In religious matters Nicholson was equally vigorous. Because of the policy of religious toleration adopted by Lord Baltimore and consistently maintained since the foundation of the colony, the members of the Established Church were probably in the minority, for Quakers, Anabaptists, Presbyterians, and Catholics had come in large numbers. In the vicinity of Annapolis the strong Puritan sentiment had died out but had been replaced by Quakerism. In 1672 George Fox, the Quaker leader, visited all parts of Maryland. In August he records in his "Autobiography" that he held "a great meeting at a place called Severn, where there was a meeting place, but not large enough to hold the people. Divers chief magistrates were at it, with many other considerable people, and it gave them generally great satisfaction."

But when the opportunity offered, the adherents of the English Church proceeded, with the support of the Governor, to organize relig-

Annapolis the Provincial Capital 35

ion in Maryland as it was arranged in the mother country. They repealed the Act of Toleration of 1649, made the Church of England the Established Church of the colony, and laid a tax of forty pounds of tobacco on every taxable person for the support of the clergy. The whole province was divided into parishes, thirty-five in all, with the land between the South River and the Severn one parish, at first called Middle Neck, later St. Anne's.

In 1699 Governor Nicholson began erecting a church on the land which had been originally assigned for the purpose and corresponding roughly to the present location of the church now standing. In 1700 the foundations were already laid, and when it was finished it was the only brick church in the colony. Communion was ordered administered at least three times each year, and no minister was to be appointed by the Governor until recommended by the Bishop of London. Clergy were to receive five shillings extra for weddings. The original building stood till just before the Revolution. Then it had become so dilapidated that a new structure was projected and the old building pulled down. When the war prevented the work being done, the town existed without a place for Episcopal worship until 1792.

The general trend of legislation in these years immediately following the English Revolution was to make Maryland a replica of England herself. As at home, Catholics were disfranchised but toleration extended to the Protestant dissenters and the Quakers. At first under the influence of the struggle with James II severe penalties were imposed on the activities of Catholic priests. They were forbidden to baptize, say mass, or exercise any other function of a priest. Even the education of children by them was forbidden. Later, however, they were allowed to officiate in private houses, which accounts for the private chapels found in such homes as that of the Carrolls in Annapolis. And in 1723 the Assembly finally adopted the same laws for religious matters as prevailed in England.

In connection with the establishment of regular parish churches in the colony occurred the visit of Dr. Thomas Bray, who was appointed in 1694 as the representative of the Bishop

Annapolis the Provincial Capital 37

of London. He is probably responsible for the communion silver which was presented to St. Anne's in 1695 by William III, whose arms may still be observed on them. But Bray's chief interest for us lies in the fact that he established in Annapolis the first public library in the colonies. Before coming to the New World Dr. Bray visited the Princess Anne and persuaded her to contribute £400 for the purchase of books to be circulated among the Maryland clergy. These volumes were inscribed with the words "Annapolitan Library," and were for some years the largest collection of books in the colonies. Of the original 1095 volumes which were sent to Maryland and distributed among the various parishes, although the larger part remained in Annapolis, St. John's College still possesses 398, and some others also have survived.

Another noteworthy event was when Dr. Bray, who remained only six months in all in America, summoned all the clergy of the province to assemble in Annapolis on May 23, 1700. This was the first ecclesiastical convention in the Colonies and inaugurated Maryland's first missionary effort,—work among the Quakers of Pennsylvania!

Governor Sir Francis Nicholson, to whom Annapolis owes so much for its elevation to the dignity of being the provincial capital and for the very plan on which its streets and public buildings were constructed,—a plan which still is in force,—was probably connected with colonial administration more widely than any other official of his time. He began as Deputy-Governor of New York, and then served as Governor of Virginia, Maryland, Nova Scotia, and South Carolina. His admiration for a heroic deed wherever performed is strikingly displayed when he sends to Hannah Dustin, the woman settler of Haverhill, Massachusetts, who escaped from Indian captivity on the banks of the Merrimac in New Hampshire by seizing a tomahawk and scalping a whole party of Indians as they slept, a pewter tankard in recognition of her Jael-like heroism. This was in 1697, while he was in Annapolis as Maryland's chief magistrate.

In 1708 Annapolis achieved further distinction by being made a corporate city with a charter and a regularly organized municipal government. This was during the administration of Governor Seymour, to whom credit is due, and not to Queen Anne, as is often asserted. As early as 1704 he seems to have proposed to the Assembly that a charter be given the town, but, as no action had been taken after four years, the Governor himself granted the city a charter in the name of the Queen and by virtue of the general authority vested in him as a Royal governor. But as the charter granted the inhabitants the right to send two delegates to the Assembly and also seemed to make it possible for the city to levy tolls and taxes on goods brought within its boundaries, the Assembly that next met took great offense at the Governor's action. In the end a compromise was effected. The Assembly conceded the Governor's right to grant the charter without consulting them or receiving specific instructions from the Crown, but the charter was amended so that the authority of the Corporation was limited to the inhabitants of the town and could be used to tax only small amounts of goods brought in. Also in view of the fact that members of the Assembly elected by the city would be at slight expense in attending, it was provided that they should be paid only one half what was given others.

The city government was organized on ancient English models; it included the Mayor, a person learned in the law, who was known as the Recorder, six Aldermen, and ten Common Councilmen. In connection with the two market days authorized weekly they were given power to hold a "Court of Pypowdry," an old English tribunal held on market days, where disputes were settled immediately in order not to detain persons who came to buy or sell, or as the original Latin phrase reads, "as speedily as dust can fall from the foot."

When in 1715 the rights of the family of Lord Baltimore were finally recognized by George I, and the province given back to the control of the fifth Lord Baltimore, who secured it chiefly because the family had now become Protestant, there was no danger of any change in the location of the capital. As stated in the charter of the city, it now excelled all other towns and ports in the province and had become the "chief mart of the whole country." From a description of about 1700 we read:

"There are about forty dwelling houses in it; seven or eight of which afford a good lodging and accommodations for strangers. There is also a State House and a Free School, built of brick, which make a great show among a parcel of wooden houses; and the foundation of a church is laid, the only brick church in Maryland."

CHAPTER IV

A CITY OF WEALTH AND FASHION

IN spite of the efforts of Governor Nicholson and the enthusiasm of the Assembly to make Annapolis a fitting capital city for the province, it is evident that in 1708 the town had many features that savored more of the frontier than of London and was quite unlike, at least in its appearance and life, the elegant little provincial center of the middle years of the century. Though Anne Arundel was already the richest and most populous county, Governor Blackiston complained that there was no house provided for the Governor and that necessaries were much dearer in Annapolis than elsewhere.

A famous satire of the early days of the century also hints at a town of few beauties. This is "The Sot-Weed Factor" (The Tobacco Buyer), by Ebenezer Cook, published in London in 1708. Cook was the son of an English captain who made frequent voyages to Maryland and was himself a resident for some years

A City of Wealth and Fashion

as Deputy Receiver General for the Baltimores. Writing in his poem, from personal experience, perhaps, he tells of reaching Maryland, visiting a rude settlement where everybody becomes drunk at the tavern, of being robbed of his clothes, and finally of being swindled out of all his money by a Quaker on the Eastern Shore. He thereupon travels to Annapolis to secure restitution by a law suit.

Of the town he says, in the Hudibrastic style in which he writes,

> "Up to Annapolis I went,
> A city situate on a plain,
> Where scarce a house will keep out rain.
> The buildings framed of cypress rare
> Resemble much our Southwark Fair.
> But stranger here will scarcely meet
> With market place, exchange, or street.
> And if the truth I must report,
> 'Tis not so large as Tottenham Court."

In the end he loses his case before a biased and drunken court.

Though William Parks, the Annapolis printer, remarked, when he reprinted the poem in 1731, that it was a description of the town twenty years earlier and did not agree with the condition of affairs later, there was evidently some truth in the picture. To one accustomed to the neatness and uniformity of English towns, except for the distinction between the gentlemen, tradesmen, and laborers,—the motley crowds at taverns and markets in Maryland must have seemed crude and uncivilized. Indians were plentiful, and those from the Eastern Shore, who had been civilized and Christianized, might often be seen on the streets. The toleration of all sects brought in Quakers in their distinctive garb; Scots came in large numbers, as did Irish, both Catholic and Protestant. Many Germans were also attracted, and in 1755 three shiploads of poor Acadians were landed in Annapolis and scattered through the province, most of them going to Baltimore. Many black slaves were also imported.

The need of labor, and Lord Baltimore's offer to give as high as one hundred acres of land to any one bringing in a servant, resulted in the arrival of indentured servants and convicts in large numbers. Hardly a ship arrived without its load of twenty to fifty men and women who were to be sold off for from two to

A City of Wealth and Fashion

five years to pay for the money advanced for their passage. These reached their height about the middle of the century.

The importation of convicts continued up to the Revolution. In 1736 one shipload of 105 convicted felons from Newgate, Marshalsea, and various county jails reached Annapolis. While many of these were not real criminals, but had been imprisoned for debt or were the victims of the harsh criminal statutes of the time, many others were the worst characters and did nothing to increase the wealth or prosperity of the colony. Severe penalties were imposed upon indentured servants who ran away from their masters; if caught, they were condemned to still longer servitude or sent to labor in the iron mines of western Maryland.

With a population in the middle of the century which was one-third negro slaves, many social difficulties arose that gave the colony anything but the appearance of a well organized and respectable English town. Laws even had to be passed dooming to perpetual slavery all offspring of marriages between white women and negroes, and providing severe punishment for any clergyman who performed such marriages.

The insecurity of the life of the Maryland plantation owner, and even of the townsman, is picturesquely displayed by the following letter written in 1739 by Stephen Bordley, a young Annapolis lawyer, to his friend Matthew Harris. It reads:

"We have lately discovered a conspiracy among the negroes in Prince George County to rise and massacre all the inhabitants on this shore, and the [scheme] was as well laid as any of the kind that I ever heard of. They were on a Sunday appointed to meet at a particular place to the number of two hundred, and after having chosen their several officers (the first thinker of this mischief having been all along agreed by them to be their king) they were to disperse every one to their several houses and there to stay till after the families in the county were abed, when they were to destroy all those of their several families, negro women and all, except the young white women only, whom they intended to keep for their wives.

"By [seizure] of the several arms which they

A City of Wealth and Fashion 47

would pick up in each family and their masters' horses and furniture they were immediately to repair to the field where the consultation was to be held, and, when a sufficient number of them was got together, they were to ride in the night immediately up to Annapolis. And dividing into two parties, one was to secure the Powder House and the other the Council Room; which when they had done and sufficiently fortified themselves with arms and ammunition, they were to dispose in several bodies over the town and cut the throats of men, women, and children, excepting none but the white young women; which when they had done (as they expected and no doubt but they would) all the negroes far and near would flock into them, they were then to dispose again into the country in large bodies and to cut off all the surviving families, and when they had done this job they intended to return to town with their young white wives and dividing the houses among themselves were to settle their government, laws, and upon the first opportunity to dispatch all the boats they could over to your [Eastern] shore to bring over such negroes as would be willing to join them.

"And in case they heard of any considerable head being made against them from your shore or other shores so that they could not keep these parts, they were to pack up all worth carrying and depart the country with their white wives to settle back in the woods.

"The first Sunday appointed for the undertaking was so rainy that few met; among those wanting were their chiefs, and the same cause providentially put it off for two other Sundays, and in the meantime a good fellow of the number belonging to Mr. Brooke, finding they were resolved to kill his master among the rest, informed him of it, which blew up the design of them, (among whom is their king, and they say a clever and sensible fellow between 40 and 50 years old). [He is] now in the county gaol, and the sheriff daily expects eight or ten more.

"This affair had been eight months in agitation; this happy disposing has put us all upon our guard, however, and will no doubt produce some good effects among us. We are now at last contriving ways and means to secure the Council House and magazine by nightly watch—and likewise for the town—of four hardy fellows and

A City of Wealth and Fashion 49

arms and ammunition now disposed into every one's hands, and the time is come (alas the day which I never thought to see) of my being made a soldier. Col. Gale is the captain of our independent troop, Rogers of the foot. We can muster forty good horses at a quarter of an hour's warning with as many bold, daring fellows on the backs of them, and sixty foot, all completely armed.

"It is said, before the appointment of any day for the execution of the design, a negro woman lying abed in a quarter overheard several of the negro fellows talking in their country language concerning this very affair, and she accordingly told her mistress of it next morning but could not gain belief. Foolish woman that sooner than give herself the trouble of looking into the affair would run the hazard of having her throat cut; but perhaps she had a mind for a black husband."[1]

Yet the fact remains that by the year 1750 Annapolis was beginning to be known as a city different from most of the colonial towns in respect to wealth, culture, and fashion. The proc-

[1] Letter Book of Stephen Bordley in Ms. Collections, Maryland Historical Society, page 58 ff.

ess is an interesting one to trace, and the rise of the city is seen to be founded on two chief factors, its distinction as the capital of the colony and the rapid growth in wealth of Maryland from the cultivation of tobacco. The increase in population is clearly marked in the vestry records of St. Anne's, where the number of persons who pay the yearly tax of forty pounds of tobacco is recorded. In 1696 they numbered 374, in 1714 they had increased to 430, in 1717 to 504, in 1723 to 663, in 1729 to 809, and in 1768 to 1,217.

The location of Annapolis geographically made it the easiest town to reach from all parts of the province, and the legal and political activities which went on here also brought to it at some time in the year almost all the important landowners. Isolated on their estates a considerable part of the year, they rather welcomed the opportunity to travel to Annapolis for litigation, which was frequent, or to represent their county in the Assembly. Many of them made it a regular practice to spend the inclement weather of the winter in the capital city and to bring their families with them. Even if they

A City of Wealth and Fashion

did not possess a house of their own there, as did the Carrolls, hospitality was profuse and family relationships exceedingly wide.

It is also important to recognize that colonial Maryland was an exceedingly prosperous community. For the production of tobacco it had great advantages, temporary though they were. Land was plentiful and cheap, white labor was in general easily secured at a reasonable rate through the use of indentured servants, and there were also many negro slaves. With cheap food and cheap labor came prosperity, and with prosperity came the benefits of education, a higher type of hospitality and entertainment, beautiful architecture, interior decoration on an elaborate scale, better furniture, and all the refinements of life. To-day much of such a surplus would be invested in better means of transportation, public and private, or in machinery for saving labor or performing automatic operations, but in the period before the Industrial Revolution a surplus of wealth such as the tobacco fields and the rising land values brought had to be used in refining life rather than in improving its utilities.

This accounts for what seems to us the excessive desire for dress, silver plate, fine furniture, and carvings as interior decoration, as well as for the large brick mansions erected. It also accounts for the prosperity of the merchants of the colony—an important class—for the only source of these luxuries was Europe. Thus imports were large and profits great. When a merchant advertised that his price to cash buyers was only double the cost of the goods to him, what must have been his profits when goods were sold on a year's credit.

One result of prosperity was frequent and close relations with relatives and friends in England and marriages between English women and the colonials. Not only did the young men spend a good part of their boyhoods in England in school, but visits were frequent, and such cases as that of one of the Dulanys, who served for several years as an officer in the Royal Navy, were not uncommon. And a considerable part of the higher social circles of Annapolis was occupied by Englishmen who came over for a term of years as officials of Lord Baltimore and brought with them all the

A City of Wealth and Fashion 53

life, dress, and ideals of eighteenth century Britons.

Such intimate contact with the mother country naturally caused much imitation of English society, and we find most of the features of life in English towns reproduced on the streets of the colonial capital and in the homes of well-to-do Annapolitans. Eddis, an Englishman who came over in 1769 to serve in the Loan Office, which was concerned with lands, and remained till the Revolution, gives us one of the best pictures of life in the town and proves himself a charming writer of letters as well as a good observer. His "Letters from America" stand as high as literature as any description of colonial life we possess. In regard to imitation he remarks that changes in fashion in London are transplanted to the colony even sooner than they are adopted by many persons of wealth in London itself. "In short," he says, "very little difference is in reality observable in the manners of the wealthy colonist and the wealthy Briton."

Thus in Annapolis, as in London, the men of the upper class wore such huge powdered wigs with the hair falling down in great curls that their hats had to be carried under the arm. They walked with a sword clattering beside them and threatening all the time to trip them by getting between their legs. The skirts of their coats were stiffened with buckram so that they stood out like huge sails. And the convivial habits of the eighteenth century Englishman were reproduced on the banks of the Severn. Stephen Bordley, a wealthy lawyer and bachelor who had been educated abroad, had Burgundy and champagne by the cask in his cellar and bought his Madeira by the pipe. He served the very finest wines and brandies, and died, like a real English gentleman of fashion, of the gout.

The ball dress of a lady of the time in Annapolis as in London was a masterpiece which required expert assistance in donning and made the wearer able to dance only the slow, stately steps of the minuet. On her head was a pyramid of hair, surmounted by a turban or a great feather head dress, while jewelled stomachers and tightly laced stays contained her waist and encouraged fainting. The dresses had trains of taffeta fifteen yards in length, and turning was possible only with the assistance of a maid.

For such ladies and gentlemen the coach with its four or six horses was the proper accompaniment. At the time of the Revolution at least six families in Annapolis exhibited this sign of gentility, and at the races at Upper Marlboro, and doubtless at similar events in the capital, sometimes fifty such vehicles were to be seen. There were also sedan chairs in Annapolis as well as on the streets of London, for Thomas Pryse, in 1774, advertises he has "a very good coach and herald painter, that undertakes painting of coaches, chariots, or *chairs,* either in cyphers, festoons of flowers, or coats of arms."

Another sign of imitation of English life was the interest in horse racing just mentioned. As early as 1745 horse races are referred to, and soon after the Maryland Jockey Club was organized by Governor Ogle and other gentlemen of the city. Regular races were instituted, generally during the sessions of the county court, when people naturally congregated in town. Races were for four miles, so that endurance, then referred to usually as "bottom," was essential. But the horses were of fine breed and frequently imported for the purpose. The usual subscription purse was one hundred guineas. The Governors seemed to feel it incumbent on them to follow Ogle's example and usually kept a racing stable. When Selim, the first thoroughbred horse of importance bred in America, and whose blood still flows in many American turf favorites to-day, was sold in 1760, he brought £1,000.

As in Britain also, the luxuries and pleasures of life were carried to excess. Bull baiting, in which the wildest bull in the county was attacked by the fiercest and most courageous dogs of the gentlemen of the district, was generally a feature of the week devoted to horse races and court business. And cock fighting was well nigh universal. On account of the time required in raising fighting birds and the fact that fights were generally to the death, such a sport drained many a gentleman's pocketbook.

More serious than either was the excessive drinking. Liquor was cheap whether imported or manufactured in the colony. Club meetings and all social dinners were expected to end in

From an etching by E. P. Metour, by permission of E. H. Curlander, Art Dealer, Baltimore

DILAPIDATED DOCKS

A City of Wealth and Fashion

the servants assisting their masters home. After the usual dinner was over the ladies retired and the gentlemen sat and consumed bumpers of all sorts until they were at least incapable of intelligent conversation. At dedications, celebrations, and holidays there was never lacking plenty of wine for the gentlemen and rum and beer for the common people.

A striking picture of the life and hospitality of the Annapolitans just before the middle of the century is contained in the Journal of William Black, secretary of a commission from Virginia which visited Annapolis in 1744 to discuss a joint treaty with the Iroquois by the colonies of Virginia, Maryland, and Pennsylvania. The party sailed up the bay and arrived in the harbor of Annapolis on the 18th of May. They were met by the gentlemen of the town, who—

"Conducted (them) to the first tavern in the town, where they welcomed the Commissioners and the gentlemen of their levee to Annapolis with a bowl of punch and a glass of wine, and afterward waited on us to the home of the Honorable Edmund Jennings, Esq., Secretary of the Province, where we dined sumptuously."

The next morning the whole party soon proceeded to the home of Governor Bladen, where they had been invited to dinner.

"We were received," Black records, "by his Excellency and his lady in the hall, where we were an hour entertained by them, with some glasses of punch in the intervals of the discourse; then the scene changed to the dining room, where you saw a plain proof of the great plenty of the country, a table in the splendent manner set out with a great variety of dishes, all served up in the most elegant way, after which came a dessert no less curious, among the rarities of which it was composed was some fine ice cream, which, with the strawberries and milk, eat most deliciously. After this repast was over, which, notwithstanding the great variety, showed a face of plenty and neatness more than luxury or profuseness, we withdrew to the room in which we were first received, where the glass was pushed briskly around, sparkling with the choicest wines, of which the table was replenished with a variety of sorts."

Governor Bladen's wife he describes as "of middle size, straight made, black hair, and of a black complexion, much pitted with small-pox, but very agreeable. . . . She is a passionate admirer of the game of whist, which she is reckoned to play admirably well."

He visited the Assembly while it was in session, but he found it nothing but a "confused multitude, and the greater part of the meaner sort, such as make patriotism their plea but preferment their design."

The Commissioners were given a ball in the Council Room, and, here he says, "Most of the ladies of any note in the town were present and made a very splendent appearance. In a room back from where they danced were several sorts of wines, punch, and sweet meats; in this room those who were not engaged in any dancing match might either employ themselves at cards, dice, backgammon, or with a cheerful glass."

The ladies were so anxious to have the visitors dance that Black remarks facetiously that they may have had designs to test their endurance, and did continue the ball till one o'clock in the morning. At a later dancing party in a private house the gentlemen were supposed to escort their partners home, but one lady had so captivated the company that she found herself with two escorts. Yet she did not lack wit to extricate herself from the difficulty; "with the help of her heels she gave both the slip, leaving them to grope their way to where they lodged." Another gentleman, after escorting his partner home, lost his way and fell into a swamp, from which he emerged and appeared at his lodgings in mud to his knees.[1]

[1] "Penna. Magazine of History and Biography," vol. I, p. 124 ff.

CHAPTER V

CLUBS, THEATERS, AND LITERATURE

PERHAPS the feature of Annapolitan life which was most peculiar to it and which also shows this close imitation of Queen Anne and Georgian England was the clubs which sprang up before the Revolution. Fortunately extensive volumes of the records of these clubs exist still and exhibit an interest in literature, satire, and learning which one rarely associates with the period before 1775. It is a reproduction of the atmosphere of Pope's "Dunciad" with the wit retained and the bitterness left out.

The records of the Tuesday Club, which lived for ten years from 1745, are the fullest but the most unreliable, for they compose a mock-history in over 1,900 closely written pages of manuscript. The club was organized by several gentlemen of the circle close to the Governor and the Court Party, as the circle of office holders and satellites of the principal officials was called. The records pretend to derive the club directly from the Tuesday Club of Lunneric, Scotland, and claim its birth as of 1725, but this is probably merely fictitious narrative of the same sort as Washington Irving's "Knickerbocker's History of New York." It points, though, to a Scottish origin in the sense that the Scots were addicted to literary clubs and that several of the prominent members were Scots.

The club met every week in the evening at the home of some member, and while the aim was purely social, original poems and essays were read, mostly of a humorous and satirical nature. They were written with some skill, however, and frequently contain quotations from French, Latin, and even Greek. The leading spirit was Alexander Hamilton, a Scotch physician who had married into the Dulany family and was at one time Secretary to the Governor. He it was who wrote the mock-history of the club and adorned the pages with grotesque caricatures in India ink, and even copied the club songs, which were scored by another member for both harpsichord and voice. The records are written in a grave, burlesque style. Members are given Latin names to heighten the similarity to ancient histories, such as Protomusicus Thornton, evidently the chief singer. Hamilton calls himself Loquacious Scribble, Esq. This remarkable manuscript is now in the possession of the Maryland Historical Society.

The club grew rapidly until it numbered twenty-five. At first its refreshments were limited to a gammon of bacon, but later elaborate suppers were served. Liquor flowed freely, but no fresh drinks were to be mixed after eleven o'clock. The most interesting of its rules was the so-called "gelastic law," by which a member touching on a sensitive topic of religion or politics was punished by being laughed at till he desisted. One of the favorite episodes was the mock trial of a member. This was characteristic of other clubs and seems to have been very popular.

The club often entertained distinguished strangers who were visiting in town, as well as the principal lawyers, merchants, and divines, and on one occasion even Benjamin Franklin.

One of the most witty members of the club was Jonas Green, the printer of the *Maryland*

Gazette, the weekly newspaper of Annapolis from 1727 on, though its unbroken existence dates only from 1745. He was honored with five P's as his title, Poet, Printer, Punster, Purveyor, and Punch-Maker General. Conundrums were a favorite amusement at the club meetings, but the samples which have been preserved are rather tame. If the members, however, were able to guess the conundrum proposed by a member, the latter was obliged to drink a bumper to the club.

The poems of greeting and congratulation read at the meetings are rather better. On one occasion Dr. Hamilton proposed a toast to the health of the club, addressing it to the president, who is known in the records as Jole, though his real name was Cole. The poem reads:

"Wishing this ancient club may always be
Promoters of facetious mirth and glee,
And that our members all may be expert
At the great punning and conundrum art,
And that our Laureate's muse may ever warble
Our fame to last as grav'd on brass or marble,
And while gay laughter furbishes each soul,
Let each a bumper drink to noble Jole."

Clubs, Theaters, and Literature   65

The following Pindaric ode seems to have been written by Jonas Green, who was addicted to writing poetry on frequent occasions. The poem is called "A Congratulatory Pindaric Ode, addressed to the Right Honorable Master Jole, Esq., President of the ancient and honorable Tuesday Club, on his having escaped the cruel distemper of the gout, this present year 1755, by his most obedient and very humble servant the Club's Poet Laureate."

"Descend, ye muses from Parnassus hill,
 And drop nepenthe in my raptur'd quill,
  High, O High,
 Let my tow'ring genius fly!
 And in ecstatic numbers sing our joy,
 Not only that great Jole's alive,
 In seventeen hundred fifty five,
 But now, that hoary winter fast retreats
 And turns his back on spring's mild genial heats,
  And yet great Jole is found
  Vigorous, brisk, and sound,
 Nor is one precious joint possess'd
 With that worst curst tormenting pest,
  The gout, the raging gout,
 Kind Heaven at last has from his limbs kept out,
  And we, with joy again,
  Released from racking pain,

Now see him mount the chair
With firm and vigorous tread,
And sound, judicious head,
The club as he was wont to regulate,
Each law he dictates, tempers each debate,
Obedience to enforce, he sagely plies his cane."

A later organization whose records have been preserved in part was the Homony Club, organized in 1770 to meet one evening each week during the winter and once a month during the rest of the year. In this case the place of meeting was the Coffee House, one of the chief taverns of the town. Here again the dominating spirit was fun and mock-heroics. Knighthood was conferred on some members, and those desiring to join made application in a humorous poetical epistle full of puns. The following poem written by J. Clapham on his becoming poet laureate is a fair sample of the rather high literary ability of the members, who included William Eddis, whose letters have been mentioned, Rev. Jonathan Boucher, rector of St. Anne's, and later the author of a history of the American Revolution, Charles Wilson Peale, the artist and painter of Washington, William

Paca, who signed the Declaration of Independence, and others:

"Behold the mighty power of place
　　The pulpit gives to parsons' grace,
　　The bench makes judges fit;
Your Laureate, too, now dares explore
Poetic realms unknown before,
　　An ex-officio wit.

At your command he strikes the strings,
　　By Homony inspired he sings,
　　Whate'er the song be worth,
He asks no fabled muse's aid,
To deck the verse this evening paid
　　A sacrifice to Mirth.

Oh still may mirth and freedom reign
Around this gaily social train;
　　And as the rolling year
Matures the plenteous crops of corn,
May homony our board adorn,
　　And crown our suppers here.

But choose your bards of greater skill
To guide the laughter-raising quill,
And if they give such numbers birth
As make gay, humorous glee and mirth,
　　Oh then how I will clap-em."

The mock-heroic style of the club records is well illustrated by the account of how one member was punished for some pretended offense by being obliged to drink "a glass of cold water (a liquor highly prejudicial to his constitution) and also to abstain from speaking during the intolerable length of a tedious insupportable minute, which unexampled instance of clubical severity so totally defeated his valuable faculties that he remained for several minutes after the expiration of the limited time unable to charm himself or others with the irresistible music of his loquacious tongue." The club seems to have dissolved in 1772 on account of the growing political bitterness of the times.

An interesting account of the origin and history of this club is contained in a passage from the reminiscences of the Rev. Jonathan Boucher mentioned above. He writes:

"Three or four social and literary men proposed the institution of a weekly club under the title of The Homony Club, of which I was the first president. It was, in fact, the best club in all respects I have ever heard of, as the sole object of it was to promote innocent mirth and

Clubs, Theaters, and Literature 69

ingenious humor. We had a secretary, and books in which all our proceedings were recorded; and as every member conceived himself bound to contribute some composition, either in verse or prose, and we had also many mirthfully ingenious debates, our archives soon swelled to two or three folios, replete with much miscellaneous wit and fun.

"I had a great share in its proceedings, and it soon grew into such fame that the Governor and all the principal people of the country ambitiously solicited the honor of being members or honorary visitants. It lasted as long as I stayed in Annapolis, and was finally broken up only when the troubles begun and put an end to everything that was pleasant and proper." [1]

That there were other clubs is indicated by the articles in the *Gazette* during the winter of 1771-2. One writer speaks effusively and apparently ironically of the "unalterable regularity" of the proceedings of the Homony .Club, and even attempts to derive the name from a Greek word "omonoia." Another club, he states, is being formed by the young men of the town,

[1] "Notes and Queries," Series V, Vol. VI, pp. 21-2.

who intend to make their chief feature a parade through the quiet streets at midnight and other roisterous behavior. He therefore suggests to them the name of the "Drumstick Club" as appropriate. In the next issue of the *Gazette*, however, is a reply in which the writer, who hides under the *nome de plume* of "Philalethes," says that the club has already been formed, is called the Independent Club, and does not practice the drunken parades mentioned. In a later issue another correspondent jokingly proposes that the clubs devote half their sessions to having the members flatter each other, and that no wits be admitted. There are frequent references to the classic articles in the *Spectator,* where Addison gives the rules of the Two-Penny Club and Steele describes the good-fellowship which pervades the Ugly Club.

With all this interest in clubs, it is not strange that the Masonic Fraternity, which spread with amazing rapidity after 1717, when the lodges in London voted to admit men of all professions and trades as long as they were respectable, should early establish itself in Annapolis. The date is unknown on account of the loss of all

Clubs, Theaters, and Literature 71

early records, but in 1750 we find Jonas Green printing a sermon preached before the members of "the Ancient and Honorable Society of Free and Accepted Masons in the Parish Church of St. Anne, in the City of Annapolis, on Wednesday, the 27th of December, 1749." The sermon was entitled "Freedom and Love," and the preacher was William Brogden, Rector of All Hallows Church, near Annapolis.

The dedication printed in the only copy known to have survived, and to be seen in the British Museum, reveals all we know of the beginnings of Masonry in the town. It reads: "Dedicated to the Right Honorable Alexander Hamilton, M.D., Master; Mr. Samuel Middleton, and Mr. John Lomas, Wardens; and others the Worshipful Brothers and Fellows of the Ancient and Honorable Society of Free and Accepted Masons, in Annapolis; This Sermon, Preached and Published at their Request, is Dedicated by their faithful Brother and most affectionate humble Servant, William Brogden."[1] Other sermons were preached and printed in 1750 and 1753.

[1] L. C. Wroth, "A History of Printing in Colonial Maryland," p. 197.

The theater was still another activity that helped to make Annapolis a center of the finer arts of life and to give social life some of the refinement that was usually so lacking in a new and frontier community. The statement has often been made that the first theater in America was erected in Annapolis in 1752. That a theater was in existence then is indicated by the notice in the *Maryland Gazette* of June 18th in which a performance of *The Beggars' Opera* at "the new theater" is announced as to be given by "the company of comedians from Virginia." But a notice in the *Virginia Gazette* of 1736 mentions a performance of *Cato* by the students of the College of William and Mary as to be given "at the theater" in Williamsburg. Moreover, a description of the latter town about 1716 mentions a theater. In both cases it is probable that the theater was merely an improvised structure, an empty warehouse, store, or dwelling.

Contemporary records show quite clearly that the "company of comedians from Virginia" that appeared in Annapolis was substantially the same company that are discovered in Philadelphia in 1749 giving *Cato* and other plays and

Clubs, Theaters, and Literature 73

then going to New York in 1750, where they appeared in a vacant house. Apparently disbanding about July, 1751, when the last New York benefit occurred, they transferred themselves to Virginia, and from there to Annapolis in June, 1752. At least the names of the players were the same. Mr. Woodham, who is advertised in Annapolis as singing the Mason's Song in the opera, was in the original Philadelphia-New York company. Mr. Kean, who is also listed in Annapolis, was one of the managers of the original company, and Miss Osborne, the leading lady in Annapolis, is mentioned among the principal performers in New York in 1750.[1]

And the repertoire of the company in Annapolis, where they performed till December, with the exception of two months in Upper Marlborough and elsewhere, contains the same plays as were given in the other cities; namely, Addison's *Cato,* Shakespeare's *Richard III,* Centlivre's *Busybody,* Farquhar's *Constant Couple, Beaux' Stratagem,* and *Recruiting*

---

[1] Seilhamer, "History of the American Theater," vol. I, pp. 30-34.

Officer, and several farces such as Garrick's *Lying Valet* and *Miss In Her Teens* and Fielding's *Virgin Unmasked* and *Mock Doctor.*

Before the end of the season in Annapolis two other players joined the company. These were Messrs. Wynell and Herbert, who had arrived in America as part of the company of William Hallam and played in Williamsburg. As they were assigned minor parts they apparently saw a chance to better themselves by a transfer.

In 1758 the Hallam Company, now reorganized, began in New York a stage career that was to last till the Revolution. In 1760, the company reached Annapolis for a long season of which we have the full list of plays, the only complete list for any city before 1773. This was due, probably, to the fact that Jonas Green, the proprietor of the *Maryland Gazette,* was a man who leaned toward literature and was even somewhat of a poet himself. In fact, his paper published more news of the stage than any other American newspaper of its day. Not only repertoires and notices of performances, but prologues, epilogues, poems addressed to

*From a drawing by Vernon Howe Bailey
by permission of Harpers Magazine*

THE DR. JOHN SHAW HOUSE, NOW THE ELKS CLUB, AND STATE CIRCLE

the actresses, and the first dramatic criticism that ever appeared in an American journal. This criticism was in regard to Otway's *Orphan* and a dramatic satire by Garrick entitled *Lethe, or Aesop in the Shades*. For the opening performance on March 3, 1760, a local poet, probably Green himself, provided a prologue and an epilogue, both of which were printed in the *Gazette*. Referring to the refining influences of the drama, the poet says:

"See! Genius wakes, dispels the former gloom,
And sheds light's blaze, derived from Greece and Rome.
With polished arts wild passions to control:
To warm the breast and humanize the soul;
By magic sounds to vary hopes and fears;
Or make each eye dissolve in virtuous tears;
'Til sympathizing youths in anguish melt,
And virgins sigh for woes before unfelt!"

The epilogue was more sprightly and complimented the colonial ladies on their virtue.

The list of plays presented is extremely interesting. In the first place it contains almost entirely the work of dramatists who are still known and respected by students of dramatic literature. Shakespeare is represented by *Richard III, Romeo and Juliet, Othello,* and the

Merchant of Venice—here called *Jew of Venice* —and the plays of Farquhar, Rowe, Otway, Vanbrugh, Fielding, Garrick, and Cibber are included, all playwrights still well known, however little their works are read or performed. It included the cream of the Restoration with many popular and superior works from the nearer and more refined eighteenth century. In the second place the list shows a company of some ability, for they presented in two months and twenty-eight performances, eighteen distinct plays and thirteen different farces.

Already the *Gazette* had stated, "with the permission of His Excellency, the Governor, a new theater is erecting in this city which will be opened soon by a company of comedians who are now at Chestertown." This shows that David Douglass, who had married the widow of the original manager of the Hallam Company and had succeeded to the ownership, as in New York and Philadelphia, erected a special building for the performances. This points to the makeshift and temporary character of all the "theaters" erected in Annapolis during the period before 1771, when a brick

Clubs, Theaters, and Literature 77

theater of finer design and appointments was erected on land secured from the Vestry of St. Anne's Parish and probably just beyond the site of the Annapolis Savings Institution on what is now West Street. That the former theaters were on the same spot is uncertain and unlikely. We are indebted to Eddis in his "Letters from America" for the best description.

"Our new theater," he writes, "of which I gave you an account in a former letter, was opened to a numerous audience the week preceding the races. The structure is not inelegant, but, in my opinion, on too narrow a scale for its length; the boxes are commodious, and neatly decorated; the pit and gallery are calculated to hold a number of people without incommoding each other; the stage well adapted for dramatic and pantomimical exhibitions; and several of the scenes reflect great credit on the ability of the painter. I have before observed that the performers are considerably above mediocrity; therefore, little doubt can be entertained of their preserving the public favor, and reaping a plenteous harvest." [1]

[1] "Letters from America," p. 108.

It is probable that the Mr. Palmer who appeared in the Annapolis performances of the Hallam Company in 1760 was the same Mr. Palmer who, after an absence, appeared in Drury Lane Theater, London, in 1761-2 and became one of the best general actors of the time, excelling in comedy but also making his mark in parts that emphasized sarcasm and irony. Mr. Scott, another leading member, as shown by the fact that he received a benefit performance, had probably been in the original company of Murray and Kean in Philadelphia which had visited Annapolis in 1752, and it is singular that there was a Mr. Murray who also is mentioned.

The theatrical season during 1769, from the 18th of February to the 13th of June, is recorded in considerable detail in the *Maryland Gazette*. This was by the New American Company, a reorganization of the "company of comedians from Virginia," which had been present in 1752. Again it is the "new theater" that is occupied. During this season amateurs seem to have participated—evidence that the town had some dramatic talent of its own. One

Clubs, Theaters, and Literature 79

amateur played *Othello* and later *Hamlet,* and one even gave a performance on the tight-rope. In all there were thirty-seven performances, and the Annapolis public saw *Romeo and Juliet, Richard III, Othello, Hamlet, Merchant of Venice,* and *King Henry IV,* even if in Dryden's "improved" versions. Other plays given were Steele's *Conscious Lovers,* Gay's perennial favorite, *The Beggars' Opera,* and most of the works of Vanbrugh, Farquhar, Garrick, Fielding, and Cibber that have been already mentioned. A notable addition was Congreve's *Mourning Bride,* in which Mrs. Osborne was Almeria.

For the remaining years till the Continental Congress in 1774 prohibited dramatic performances, the American, or Hallam-Douglass Company, was the only dramatic resource of Annapolis. In August, 1770, it began a short but brilliant season in the Maryland capital, and visited there in each of the three years that followed.

The brightest star in the company in 1770 seems to have been Miss Hallam, for she called forth both of the poetical tributes which were printed in the *Gazette,* and which express in very capable verse the character of her charms. One reads in part as follows:

> "She speaks! What elocution flows!
> Oh! softer far the strains
> Than fleeces of descending snows
> Or gentlest vernal rains.
>
> Do solemn measures slowly move?
> Her looks inform the strings:
> Do Lydian airs invite to love?
> We feel it as she sings.
>
> Around her see the Graces play,
> See Venus' wanton doves,
> And in her eye's pellucid ray,
> See little laughing Loves.
>
> Ye Gods! 'Tis Cytherea's face;
> 'Tis Dian's faultless form;
> But hers alone the nameless grace
> That every heart can charm."

Miss Hallam's portrait was also painted by Charles Wilson Peale, the first man to paint Washington, and excited so much admiration that an admirer of the two burst forth into poetry, again in the *Gazette.* In part it reads:

Clubs, Theaters, and Literature 81

"To Mr. Peale on his painting Miss Hallam in the character of Fedele in "Cymbeline."
When Hallam as Fedele comes distressed,
Tears fill each eye and passion heaves each breast;
View with uplifted eyes the charming maid,
Prepared to enter though she seems afraid.
And see, to calm her fears and soothe her care,
Bellarius and the royal boys appear.
Thy pencil has so well the scene conveyed
Thought seems but an unnecessary aid.
How pleased we view the visionary scene,
The friendly cave and rock and mountain green;
Nature and art are here at once combined,
And all Elysium to one view confined."

Her portrayal of Imogen in *Cymbeline* also comes in for very favorable comment in the *Gazette*. An admirer, whom we suspect to be Eddis, says:

"She exceeded my utmost idea! Such delicacy of manner! Such classic strictness of expression! The music of her tongue—the *vox liquida*,—how melting. Notwithstanding the injuries it received from the horrid construction of the roof and the untoward construction of the whole house, methought I heard once more the warbling of Cibber in my ear. How true and thorough her knowledge of the part she personated! Her whole form and demeanor how happily convertible and universally adapted to the variety of her part."

Of the company in general the same critic says: "The merit of Mr. Douglass's company is notoriously in the opinion of every man of sense in America, whose opportunities give him a title to judge—take them all in all—superior to that of any company in England, except those of the metropolis."

In the field of literature, Annapolis, like the other towns of America, produced few, if any, geniuses, but displayed an interest in the current forms of polite literature which helped to refine society and even leave some works worth perusal to-day. The *Spectator* and the literary masterpieces of Queen Anne's age were to be found in the libraries of the gentlemen of the town, and the witty, satirical work of the days of Pope seemed to appeal to the *dilettanti* of the Maryland metropolis.

The "Sot-Weed Factor," that scurrilous picture of the crudeness of Colonial life in 1708 and earlier, has already been mentioned. In

1730 its author, Ebenezer Cook, published in Annapolis, "Sot-Weed Redivivus, or the Planter's Looking-Glass, In Burlesque Verse," wherein he notes the change produced in twenty years. He writes,

"Bound up for Port Annapolis,
The famous beau metropolis
Of Maryland, of small renown
When Anne first wore England's crown,
Is now grown rich and opulent,
The awful seat of Government."

In 1731 Cook again solicited public favor with another satirical poem, this time on Bacon's Rebellion, and issued another edition of the original "Sot-Weed Factor."

In 1728, one Richard Lewis began the publication of several pieces of literature while a resident of the town. The best description of him is contained in a letter written by Governor Benedict Leonard Calvert in 1729,[1] in which he says, "one Lewis, a schoolmaster here who formerly belonged to Eaton, a man really of ingenuity and in my judgment well versed in

[1] L. C. Wroth, "A History of Printing in Colonial Maryland," p. 48.

poetry." His first book was a translation of a Latin satire by an Englishman, Edward Holdsworth, entitled "Muscipula, The Mouse Trap, or the Battles of the Cambrians and the Mice." A considerable list of subscribers is printed in the volume, and thus shows some appreciation of poetry, albeit satirical. In 1732 he again appears with the "Carmen Seculare," a poetical address to Lord Baltimore on his visit to Maryland; finally in the *Gazette* of February 9, 1733, was printed a poem "A Rhapsody" by the same author. It seems probable that their author was for a time the schoolmaster of King William's School.

At the head of all the satirists and writers of mock heroics must, I believe, be placed Dr. Alexander Hamilton, the author of the amusing minutes of the Tuesday Club already mentioned. The records of the clubs show that this sort of literature was very popular, and in the circulating library which William Aikman conducted for several years on West Street in the bookshop, and which is frequently advertised in the *Gazette,* must have been many a volume of Pope and Swift. Here for a guinea a year residents of Annapolis could secure volumes for reading, certainly a moderate charge for such an opportunity. Hamilton is also noteworthy for a manuscript account of a journey he made in 1744 from Annapolis to Portsmouth, New Hampshire, and return, in which he records his actual impressions of the people and places he visited. As Dr. Upton Scott, of whom we shall hear more later, said of him in 1809, Hamilton was "a most cheerful facetious companion amongst his friends, whom he never failed to delight with the effusions of his wit, in which acquirements he had no equal. . . . Although his jokes were occasionally somewhat indelicate, and he frequently chants the pleasures of the bowl, no man exceeds him in temperance and purity of morals." [1] He can be safely named the chief of the Annapolitan wits.

The literary achievements of the Colonials depended so much upon the existence of printing presses that it is worth noting that when Governor Nicholson moved the seat of government to Annapolis from St. Mary's, the only printing

[1] Introduction to Hamilton's "Itinerarium," by Albert Bushnell Hart. The original manuscript is in the Bixby Collection, St. Louis.

press in the colony came along too, and that the first license to print was issued to a woman, Dinah Nuthead, whose husband had been the printer in the former capital and whose business she continued for a short while. It was another printer, William Parks, who in 1727 began the publication of the *Maryland Gazette,* the sixth paper in the Colonies, and which after its demise in 1728, was revived in 1745 and continued to be published under the same management till 1839. In many of its features it stands first among Colonial newspapers.

Jonas Green, the printer who laid the permanent foundations of the *Gazette's* success, and whose house still stands in Charles Street in the possession and occupancy of his descendants, was a New Englander. His great grandfather, Samuel Green, came to Boston with John Winthrop in 1630 and settled in Cambridge, where in 1649 he succeeded Day, the first printer in British America. Jonas Green himself had been born in Boston in 1712 and after serving an apprenticeship with his father in New London, Conn., where his father was in business, returned to Cambridge and carried on a business of his

Clubs, Theaters, and Literature 87

own. He later removed to Philadelphia, where he was a friend and associate of Franklin's, and in 1738 settled in Annapolis.

With the publication of the *Maryland Gazette* in 1745, Green became one of the most useful citizens of the town. Not exactly an aristocrat, he was yet associated with the Governor's circle in much the same way as Franklin seems to have had the entrèe to all classes of society. He was a clerk of entries at the Annapolis races, he was secretary of the local lodge of Masons, alderman, vestryman, and even auctioneer. We have seen his various activities in the clubs as poet, punster, etc. At his death in 1767 his widow, Anne Catherine Green, and her son continued the *Gazette* so that again a woman printer appears in Annapolitan history.

The emphasis which the *Gazette* gave to theatrical news, and its printing the first bit of dramatic criticism that appeared in an American journal, has been mentioned. But literature in Annapolis owes much to the general encouragement it received from Jonas Green. A "Poet's Corner" had its place in the scanty four pages which were devoted to news of the whole world and the advertisements of runaway servants, auction sales, arrivals of English and India goods, and official notices. Some of these verses, generally amatory, and by such swains as Philander and such maidens as Phoebe, are in the sprightly style of the poets of the Cavalier period when Herrick and Waller wrote. And political controversy was allowed with equal opportunities to both sides, even in the intense days before the Revolution.

The printing of Bacon's "Laws of Maryland" by Jonas Green in 1765 was the climax of Green's work as a printer, for he died two years later. The volume took four years to print and bind, but especially in the large folio edition on creamy paper watermarked with the seal of the province it presents "a quiet splendor, a mellow and harmonious blending of paper and types which was not surpassed in any book printed in colonial America."[1]

The other important literary character besides Green—omitting Daniel Dulany, the Younger, whose "Considerations" stands with Dickinson's

[1] Wroth, *op. cit.*, p. 110.

Clubs, Theaters, and Literature 89

"Farmer's Letters" as the height of Revolutionary political argument, and who will be discussed later—was William Eddis, author of "Letters from America," published in London in 1792 but written in Annapolis in the years between 1769 and 1777. Eddis was an Englishman who had come to Maryland as Surveyor of Customs and who remained till the last shred of British authority vanished before the movement for independence. A lover of *belle lettres,* if not a literary genius, he reflects the polished and versatile Englishman of the eighteenth century. As a picture of Annapolis in all the phases of its society and for charming appreciations of Maryland characters and scenes the letters still have literary value. His poetical tributes to the theater have been already quoted from, and in one case he wrote a prologue for a company performing in Philadelphia.

Eddis's sincere wishes for a continued peace between the Colonists and the mother country are evident throughout his letters. A poetical expression of these, where perhaps his intense feeling elevated his style and gave it the vigor it usually lacked, is worth quoting in part. It reads:

"Sea-girt Britannia! mistress of the isles!
  Where Faith and Liberty united reign;
Around whose fertile shores glad Nature smiles
  And Ceres crowns with gifts the industrious swain!

"Thy generous, daring sons have nobly toil'd
  To guard thy cliffs from arbitrary sway;
In well fought fields the baffled tyrant foil'd,
  Where glorious Freedom led the arduous way!

"Now through the land Dissention stalks confest,
  With foul Distrust and Hatred in her train;
The dire infection runs from breast to breast,
  And statesmen plan—and patriots plead in vain!

"All-gracious Heaven, avert the impending storm;
  Bid every jealous jarring faction cease;
Let sweet Content resume her lovely form,
  And o'er the land diffuse perpetual peace.

"And, when again our colours are unfurl'd,
  May Britons nobly join one common cause!
With rapid conquests strike the wondering world,
  In firm support of Liberty and Laws." [1]

In one other aspect of the fine arts, Annapolis deserves a brief mention. This is in painting.

[1] Pp. 138-9.

John Hesselius, son of a Swedish missionary who finally settled in Philadelphia and accumulated a competence, came to Annapolis about 1763 and married an Annapolis lady. He had studied under pupils of Sir Godfrey Kneller and painted many of the family portraits to be found still hanging in the homes of native Marylanders.

Better known is Charles Wilson Peale, a native of the Eastern Shore who came to Annapolis at the age of thirteen as an apprentice. In the course of the following years he acquired the arts of a silversmith, saddler, taxidermist, watchmaker, coachmaker, dentist, engraver, and painter. His promising dexterity interested a group of wealthy Marylanders and he was sent to Boston to study under Copley and later to learn painting from West in London. It is said that he secured his first knowledge of painting from John Hesselius, to whom he promised one of his best saddles if he would let him see him paint a picture. On his return to Annapolis he painted many portraits, and was the first artist to make a portrait of Washington, who sat at Mount Vernon in 1772.

CHAPTER VI

SOME TORY FAMILIES AND THEIR HOMES

AROUND the shores of Chesapeake Bay and the rivers and inlets which are tributary to it stand to-day more representatives of the life of Colonial times than are to be found in any other area of equal size. The men and the women of those days are gone and many of them sleep in unmarked and forgotten graves, but the Colonial houses, nearly a thousand in number, still survive to give us an actual touch with the life of the past. In Annapolis are probably found more of the more pretentious of these homes than can be seen in any other one place. Because the town has had little commercial, and almost no industrial, development since the end of the Revolution there has been little need to tear down ancient mansions to accommodate the spread of business and industry.

In many cases the mansion which the family occupied has been the chief reason for keeping alive the memory of its builders, for so beautiful was the structure raised in the prosperous days when land was cheap, labor plentiful, and the favors of the Lord Proprietary frequent that to-day it draws from all parts of the country a succession of visitors and admirers. To step into one of these Colonial mansions with its high ceilings, its wonderful carving, and its absolute purity and simplicity of design, is to draw a breath of the pure, pristine air of a golden age. It will be worth while, therefore, to linger a while in the homes of the principal characters in the life of Annapolis before the Revolution, learn their histories, and estimate their service in creating the ideals of America to-day. It is in this last feature that all genealogical study and historical interest find their justification. And it will be seen that, divided though they were when the Revolution came into what may be called the parties of the Tories and the patriots, there was not a clear cleavage between the two either in education, manners, or wealth. And the old houses that they have left us are about equally divided between the two groups.

In a colony where, as in Maryland, the whole area had originally belonged to one man, the

Proprietary, and was his to give away or sell as he pleased, it was natural that those close to him or who served his interests faithfully should be bountifully rewarded. This generally took the form of very extensive grants of uncleared land or lucrative offices in the government of the colony. Where both were secured the fortunate family found it easy to establish itself.

In the period from about 1730 to the breaking out of the movement for independence, a few families almost wholly comprehended the ruling class as far as the power of the Lord Baltimores went. In 1742 Thomas Bladen, a native of Maryland but a relative by marriage of the Lord Baltimore then living, for they had married sisters, became Governor, and his descendants, either directly or by marriage alliances, occupied the offices of government and were the leaders of what was facetiously called the "Court Party" for many years afterwards.

Perhaps the chief episode of Governor Bladen's administration was his effort to erect a fitting residence for the Governors of the province. In 1744 he purchased four acres of land on what is now the campus of St. John's College and received from the Assembly funds for starting the construction of a Governor's mansion. He secured the services of Simon Duff, a Scottish architect, and pushed the work until, when the foundations and side walls had been raised and the roof was almost completed, the Assembly, thinking the Governor extravagant, refused to appropriate the money needed to finish the work. Although practically all the materials were on hand, the deadlock continued until the structure fell into a dilapidated state and the loose pieces of ornament stored in the basement were stolen. Not till 1784 was anything done, and then the Legislature turned the property over to St. John's College for its chief building. By them it was completed, and stands to-day in appearance as it was in Colonial days, —since when the interior and roof were devastated by fire in 1909 the reconstruction was on the old lines and the foundations and part of the side walls were retained. But Bladen's name was chiefly commemorated for many years by its nickname—"Bladen's Folly."

Governor Bladen's sister Ann married Benjamin Tasker, who already had received large grants of land from Lord Baltimore and who was President of the Governor's Council for many years, and acted as Governor whenever that official was absent from the province or when the office was vacant. Their daughter married Samuel Ogle, a captain of cavalry in the British Army who had been sent out in 1731 as Governor and who also served a second term from 1747 to his death in 1752. In this last administration he occupied the gray brick mansion on the corner of King George Street and College Avenue he may have built. Its beautiful box hedges and arched doorway at the side still remain. It is related that so great was the Governor's love for horses that he even placed his stables along the walk leading to the main entrance so that he might more easily see his pets as he entered or left his house.

When Governor Ogle married the eighteen-year-old Ann Tasker in 1741, he became about the climax of wealth and aristocracy. From his father-in-law he had bought an estate, Belair, about twenty miles from Annapolis, and there, on a 3600-acre plantation with 600 acres of deer park, a race track, kennels, bowling green, and

Some Tory Families 97

the four-in-hand coach with outriders in which he and his bride made the journeys to and from Annapolis, he maintained all the traditions of the English Tory gentleman with perhaps larger resources than most of them possessed.

Another daughter of President Tasker, as he was generally known, married Daniel Dulany, Jr., and helped to add to the strength of this latter family's connections with the circle about the Governor. The elder Dulany was already one of the leading officials of the province. He had originally come to Maryland from Ireland as an indentured servant, although he had studied at Trinity College. So favorably did he impress his purchaser, a wealthy land owner, George Plater, that he released him, sent him to Gray's Inn, London, for a legal education, and even approved his allying himself in marriage with one of his family. After Dulany removed to Annapolis in 1721 he rose rapidly and became in quick succession Alderman, Councillor, and Recorder of the City, and then Attorney-General, Judge of Admiralty, Commissary-General, Agent and Receiver-General, as well as a member of the Governor's Council.

Though he at first was a leader of the party opposed to the Proprietary and the Governor, he changed his position in Ogle's time and became a strong Tory.

Daniel Dulany, the Younger, was, like other well-to-do Annapolis youths, sent abroad for his education. After graduating from Eton, and attending Clare Hall, Cambridge, he entered the Temple for the study of law. When he returned to his native colony in 1747 and was admitted to the bar, his family and official connections as well as his unusual ability soon brought a very extensive law practice and a membership in the Governor's Council as well as the position as Secretary of the Province. Though thus closely connected with "Government," he nevertheless made his greatest reputation in 1765 when he published a pamphlet opposing the right of Parliament to impose a stamp act on the colonies. This was his famous "Considerations." It was first printed in Annapolis, but soon issued in London, and was referred to and used by William Pitt in his speeches in Parliament in defense of the American contentions. It has been said of it: "A Maryland lawyer had turned from

Some Tory Families 99

leading the bar of a province to set up a true theory of the constitution of an empire with the dignity, the moderation, the power, the incommunicable grace of a great thinker and genuine man of letters."[1]

When the actual opposition to British authority was discussed in 1774, Dulany, however, held back, remained loyal to the Crown, and was easily the most distinguished Loyalist in Maryland. As a result he was proclaimed a traitor, his property confiscated, and he forced to spend the rest of his days in obscurity. He died in 1791.

Other members of the Dulany family who held offices in the government were Walter Dulany, who also occupied the lucrative offices of Commissary-General and Secretary. Walter, Jr., loyal in the Revolution, joined a regiment of American supporters of the King, went to England, and did not return till some years after the war closed. Another Dulany, Lloyd, was the owner of the square, lofty town house which is now the Masonic Temple on Conduit Street. Its imposing height, its beautiful cornice, and

[1] Woodrow Wilson, "A History of the American People," vol. III, p. 87.

the header bond brickwork make it still an impressive structure. Lloyd Dulany had a tragic history that recalls the careers of many young English aristocrats of the eighteenth century. The youngest son of Daniel Dulany, the Elder, he adhered to the King in the Revolution, was forced to flee to England, and had his house taken away from him for treason. In London he ran across the notorious Rev. Bennett Allen, at one time Rector of St. Anne's in Annapolis, and about the rascalliest parson ever sent to Maryland by the Baltimores. In spite of the fact that Allen's dissoluteness was known, the orders of Lord Baltimore to the Governor had to be carried out, and he was given a parish. In Annapolis he became involved in a dispute with one of the Dulanys, Walter, and was caned by him on the street. When he encountered Lloyd Dulany in London, he provoked a quarrel with him and in the duel that ensued killed him.

It was Walter Dulany who acquired the Dulany home which stood till 1883 within the Naval Academy grounds on what is now the site of Bancroft Hall, the midshipmen's quarters. The house had a charming location on a

Some Tory Families 101

point which separated the Severn from the harbor of Annapolis and gave an unobstructed view of the Chesapeake and Kent Island beyond. The original owner and builder had been Simon Duff, who sold it to Walter Dulany in 1753. Though his property was confiscated in 1781 because of his adherence to the British cause, the family retained the house till 1808. In that year it was acquired with the adjoining property by the Federal Government as a location for Fort Severn and was occupied by the commander of the fort till 1845. When in that year the Naval Academy was given the property it became the residence of the Superintendent, and so remained till 1883, when it was condemned as unsafe and torn down. Few dwellings in the town have thus had more distinguished occupants.

Another member of the official circle was responsible for the pretentious mansion in the residential quarter—between the State House and the Severn—where the Governors lived for nearly a century. This was Edmund Jennings, Secretary of the Province and a member of Lincoln's Inn, who married a Maryland widow and finally died in the province. He it was who erected the central portion of the rather imposing house which stood near the Dulany mansion and is usually referred to as the "old Governor's mansion." When a few years after its erection Governor Horatio Sharpe arrived, he rented it and thus began its career as the home of Maryland's chief executives. When Sharpe was succeeded by Governor Eden in 1769 the latter bought the property and added a wing on each side of the main building. In this form, with a spacious salon stretching across the rear of the main house and with a beautiful garden extending down toward the Severn, one can imagine it as Colonel Washington spent the night here with his friend, Governor Eden, or, as Winston Churchill fictitiously but realistically pictures it, when Richard Carvel arrived with his grandfather in his barge rowed by ten negro boatmen to consult with Eden and the other members of the Council about the disorders over the Stamp Act.

When the Revolution came, the house with the rest of the Governor's property was confiscated. The house was then assigned to the first

Some Tory Families 103

Governor under the new constitution, and occupied in turn by practically all his successors until 1869, when the land about was added to the Naval Academy and the building made the Academy Library. In 1901, just before the extensive rebuilding of the Academy, it was torn down.

Another official of the Proprietary Government was Thomas Jennings, Chief Clerk of the Land Office, always a lucrative position. He was a cousin of the famous Sarah Jennings, the confidant of Queen Anne and the first Duchess of Marlborough. He was only nineteen when he came to Maryland but seems to have returned to England to study law and rose to be Attorney-General of the province. He is responsible for two fine Colonial houses that still stand, the Jennings House on Prince George Street opposite Carvel Hall and the Brice House at the corner of East Street and Prince George Street. When his daughter Julianna married Colonel James Brice in 1745 Jennings had already erected for them as a wedding gift the magnificent Brice House.

The Jennings House is without distinguishing traits and has even lost a wing which was included in the original structure, but the Brice House stands out as a monarch among the insignificant structures that now surround it. It faces the harbor and has a beautifully cut cornice along its front facade. Its huge chimneys rise to an impressive height and as one approaches the house through the narrow street which gives access to it from the Naval Academy the chimneys and the gables stand boldly out against the sky.

The interior is rich in carving, and has a staircase of San Domingo mahogany. The state drawing room at the rear of the house is a spacious apartment with beautiful cornices of carved woodwork, a fireplace surrounded with delicate carving, and a mantel supporting a plaster panel of impressive size and with a carved frame. Here the entertainments, at some of which Washington is said to have been present, were doubtless in harmony with the sumptuous surroundings. Of its first mistress memory chiefly centers around a sort of cake, called Naples biscuit, which she was famous for dispensing.

The Scott House on Shipwright Street keeps

Some Tory Families 105

alive the name of another associate of the Governors of the pre-Revolutionary time, Dr. Upton Scott, who seems not to have had any difficulty in adjusting himself to the changed conditions after independence was gained. He built the house which now stands at the top of a slope leading down to the water of Spa Creek and not far from the home of Charles Carroll of Carrollton. In fact, both are now the property of the Catholic Church and are used respectively for the priests and for the teaching Sisters of the parish.

Dr. Scott came to Annapolis in 1753 with Governor Sharpe, and about 1760 built this house. In a rear room Governor Eden died in 1784. Its hall is probably the most beautiful in the city. It is sometimes spoken of as the best "local habitation" for the town house of Richard Carvel's grandfather on Marlboro Street, as Churchill calls it. But as any student of the early history of the city will recognize as he reads the story of Richard Carvel, Churchill has done exactly as he maintained after its publication—drawn a composite and entirely fictitious picture of the geography of the town and used the materials on which any historical story of Colonial Annapolis must rest with an entirely free hand. The atmosphere of the book is accurate and the details mentioned reasonably credible but there is no pretense to anything more.

About equally distant from the homes of Dr. Scott and Charles Carroll of Carrollton stands another house, on Duke of Gloucester Street, which also owes its erection to another of the "Court Party." In 1753 Governor Sharpe brought with him as a secretary John Ridout, whose rapid rise to affluence and office well illustrates the political and social conditions of an almost autocratic provincial government. He came to Maryland at the age of twenty-one after six years at Oxford, where he had distinguished himself in the classics. Four years later he acquitted himself well in a mission to the Indians and in 1760 had become a member of the Governor's Council.

When in 1765 he had thus made a place for himself in the colony, he married Mary Ogle, daughter of the late Governor, secured a considerable fortune, and united himself with almost

Some Tory Families 107

all of the Court circle. Mary Ogle's harpsichord, a wedding gift, still stands in the house he then built. As planned, the house faces toward the east, its garden in Colonial days extending down to the waters of the harbor and presenting a striking appearance when viewed from that side. To-day the opposite doorway on Duke of Gloucester Street is more often seen, and in its simplicity has a charm all its own. On the water side a fine portico projects from the main entrance and above are beautiful Palladian windows. Here again Washington frequently dined or stayed over night on his visits to Annapolis before he and his friend had to choose between King and Colony. In the Revolution John Ridout took no part but remained in Maryland in obscurity till hostilities had ceased. The beautiful estate of Whitehall, built by Governor Sharpe eight miles out of town, became his on the death of the Governor, and even in the face of the Confiscation Act John Ridout managed to save both town and country homes by an exchange for some property in Ireland.

But the fate of most of the Maryland Loyalists was not so happy. Their families were scattered, they were often unable to communicate with them during the war, their correspondence was opened and read, their property taken away, and the compensation they received from the British authorities meager. Yet most of them either remained in Maryland on obscure estates or returned as soon as peace had been proclaimed, and tried to adapt themselves to the new conditions. And it is creditable to the patriots to notice that the wounds of such a bitter difference of opinion were not long in passing away.

CHAPTER VII

THE THREE SIGNERS OF THE DECLARATION OF INDEPENDENCE AND THEIR ANNAPOLIS HOMES

NOT the least of the attractions of Annapolis to the student of American history is the fact that it contained among its citizens three of the fifty-six signers of the Declaration of Independence, and that the town house of each of them still stands. It is doubtful if this can be said of any other city in the country. Perhaps the most famous of their group, these men were, however, but part of a brilliant and devoted band of patriotic lawyers, merchants and land-owners who inspired and controlled the movement for greater freedom in the affairs of government and greater opportunities for all.

Of the three Signers, Charles Carroll of Carrollton was easily the outstanding figure. The differences in his circumstances as related to the events of his time are really striking. He is not all that we generally include in our conception of a Revolutionary patriot. He was a Catholic, as all his family were and have remained. He was the richest individual in the Colonies. He was, until a new Constitution was adopted, ineligible to vote in any election. He was almost European in his education and ideas, as he had spent seventeen years of his youth on the Continent and in London. Yet he was heart and soul in sympathy with the patriot cause, and gave unsparingly of his time and wealth to help it achieve success.

The grandfather of Charles Carroll of Carrollton, also named Charles, had originally arrived in the province with a commission from Lord Baltimore, with whom he was intimately connected, as Attorney-General, an office in the gift of the Proprietary. But no sooner had he reached Maryland than the authority of Lord Baltimore was abrogated by William of Orange and the position vanished. Yet he administered so well the business with which he was thereupon entrusted that by 1707 he had received 60,000 acres of land. In the same year he received the 10,000 acre tract which he later called Dougheregan Manor, and a little later 10,000 more, which

Signers and Their Homes 111

he named Carrollton, and from which the Signer derived his distinctive designation. Thus he laid the foundation for what became in the wise care of his son, generally known as Charles Carroll of Annapolis, the largest fortune in America and which was estimated to amount before the Revolution to at least $2,000,000.

Charles Carroll of Annapolis, father of the Signer, was educated abroad and took over the management of the family estate at the age of twenty-one. The house in which he lived, and where his son also had his residence whenever in Annapolis, still stands on the banks of Spa Creek and presents its original condition. The house was built by the father of the Signer, and the story is that buying the land from a widow he paid many times its real value in order to do her a kindness she would receive in no other way. Parts of the building date back as far at least as 1735. There, in a part of the town not originally set aside for gentlemen's residences, but somewhat apart from the rest of the principal inhabitants—a position which the Carrolls seem always to have occupied—the family homestead was established. Later Dougheregan Manor became the principal center of the family life, but it was at Annapolis that the Carrolls, including the Signer, who was born here in 1737, were found on all important occasions. The gigantic tree which stood near the house saw Washington often entertained here, and in 1783, when he resigned his commission as commander-in-chief, the whole community celebrated on this spot at the expense of Charles Carroll of Carrollton.

Of the many letters exchanged between Charles Carroll of Carrollton and his father while the former was abroad securing an education, perhaps the most revelatory of the character of the father is a part of a letter written in 1756 in which he describes the situation of the Acadians who had been deported from Nova Scotia and scattered along the Atlantic seaboard in the English colonies. He says:

"It has been the misfortune of 900 and odd of these poor people to be sent to Maryland, where they have been entirely supported by private charity and the little they can get by their own labor, which for want of employment has been but a poor resource to them. Many of them have met with very humane treatment from the

*From a drawing by Vernon Howe Bailey
by permission of Harpers Magazine*

THE CARROLL HOUSE, NOW ST. MARY'S RECTORY, BIRTHPLACE
OF CHARLES CARROLL OF CARROLLTON

Roman Catholics here, but a real or pretended jealousy inclined this government not to suffer them to live with Roman Catholics. I offered the government to take and support two families consisting of fourteen souls, but was not permitted to do it.

"These poor people for their numbers were perhaps the most happy of any on the globe. They manufactured all they wore, and their manufactures were good; they raised in great plenty the provisions they consumed; their habitations were warm and comfortable; they were all upon a level, being all husbandmen, and consequently as void of ambition as human nature can be. They appear to be very regular and religious, and that from principle and a perfect knowledge of their duty, which convinces me that they were blessed with excellent pastors. But alas, how is their case altered! They were at once stripped of everything but the clothes on their backs: many have died in consequence of their sufferings, and the survivors see no prospect before them but want and misery." [1]

In these letters we trace the migrations of

[1] K. M. Rowland, "Life of Charles Carroll of Carrollton," vol. I, pp. 27-8.

young Carroll through various Jesuit schools at St. Omer, Rheims, Paris, and Bourges, and in his studies in law at the Temple in London, where he spent three or four years. Thus when he returned to Annapolis in 1765, he was thoroughly at home with civil law in all its phases and had seen enough of English and Continental society to feel thoroughly at ease in any of the circles of Annapolis. Yet the whole impression we derive from his letters and from the character sketches of him made by various individuals is that he ever retained a certain simplicity which never made him ambitious for the leadership of society or for the exhibition of his wealth. When he appeared in Philadelphia at the session of the Continental Congress he at once drew from John Adams the following favorable "character:"

"A gentleman of independent fortune—perhaps the largest in America—a hundred and fifty or two hundred thousand pounds sterling; educated in some university in France, though a native of America; of great abilities and learning, complete master of the French language, and a professor of the Roman Catholic religion;

Signers and Their Homes 115

yet a warm, a firm, a zealous supporter of the rights of America, in whose cause he has hazarded his all."[1]

As a person excluded by religion from any active political rôle, but trained in the principles of government and law more deeply than perhaps any other Marylander of his generation, it was natural that when opposition developed to the existing government, based upon the supremacy of Protestantism and the Parliament as it was, Carroll should take the side of the reformers and seek political freedom at their hands. And it was also natural that they should welcome the assistance of the wealth and following which he represented. His championship of the popular cause in the fee controversy of 1773, as will be related in the next chapter, quickly made him a member of all the important committees which directed the growing opposition to the mother country. This finally sent him to the Continental Congress and gave him many important posts of a business nature during the Revolution. As a leading Catholic and a master of French he was sent with Franklin, Samuel

[1] *Ibid.*, p. 145.

Chase, and John Carroll, a cousin who was a priest in the Catholic Church, on a mission to the inhabitants of Quebec to secure their assistance in the revolutionary cause. After the war he became United States Senator from Maryland, was active in all the chief enterprises of the day, and when he died in 1832 the last surviving signer of the famous Declaration passed away.

He was, it has been said, the first to append his signature, the richest man who signed, the only Catholic who signed, and the last one of the Signers to die. But the commonly accepted story that as he wrote his name some one remarked, "I see several millions gone through confiscation," but another said "Oh, there are several Charles Carrolls," and that then Carroll added "of Carrollton," is obviously untrue, since from the time when he returned from abroad and assumed an active part in the affairs of the family he consistently penned his name in this way.

The best known of houses of Signers is probably least frequently associated with its builder and the Declaration of Independence. This is

Signers and Their Homes 117

the structure on Prince George Street which constitutes the western half of the Carvel Hall Hotel. The name is, of course, derived from Winston Churchill's novel, but there the building serves as the home of Dorothy Manners. But the house is historically the former residence of William Paca, where he lived from 1763 till 1780. A native of the Eastern Shore of Maryland, he first attended Franklin's College of Philadelphia, and after graduating went to the Middle Temple in London to study law. In the beginning of his legal practice in Annapolis he was associated with Stephen Bordley, one of the leaders of the bar, until he was admitted to practice in 1764. When he married Mary Chew a year before this he seems to have erected the house that still stands to recall his career.

The house is plainer in its interior decorations than some of its contemporaries, but in Colonial times its attractiveness was enhanced by beautiful gardens which extended down to a little inlet running from behind the house to the harbor. Here were box bordered walks, beautiful garden plots, an octagonal summer house, a miniature lake, a fountain, and a wharf at the water's edge.

Here lay anchored the roomy barge in which the master of the house was rowed by half a dozen or more negro slaves in livery on his visits to relatives and friends along the Severn. Enough of this beauty remained till Winston Churchill's midshipman days at the Naval Academy and the months he spent living in this very house while writing the novel that made his reputation to induce him to give the house a prominent place in the story.

William Paca's activities in behalf of the patriot cause were as varied and important as any other Marylander's. He was early a member of the Sons of Liberty, the organization that enforced the non-importation agreement; he headed the body of citizens which showed its abhorrence of the Stamp Act by hanging in effigy the Stamp Distributor and then burying the proclamation in a coffin. In the Continental Congress, to which he was sent as a delegate from 1774 to 1778, he early advocated independence, even in advance of the wishes of his constituents. He was one of the three Maryland delegates—the fourth being absent—who voted for the adoption of the Declaration of Independence on July

Signers and Their Homes 119

4th, and one of the four who affixed their signatures to the engrossed document on August 2d.

In home affairs Paca was also incessantly active. He had been in 1774 a member of the Committee of Correspondence which practically ruled the colony during that uncertain period, was frequently consulted when the new State government was formed, was appointed one of the principal judges, and from 1782 to 1786 served as Governor. In December, 1789, Washington nominated him as Judge of the United States District Court of Maryland and he served in this capacity till his death ten years later, the same year in which his illustrious chief passed away.

Not far from the Paca House another Signer built a mansion for himself, and, curiously enough, the most vehement of the popular party against the aristocratic Tories is remembered in Annapolis for the most pretentious of all the Colonial mansions that have survived. Few of the old houses possessed a full third story, and the chief one of this type was erected by Samuel Chase, another lawyer, a man of purely Maryland birth and education, and the firebrand of all the popular movements that preceded the Revolution. He was referred to by his opponents as "a busy body, a restless incendiary, a ringleader of mobs, a foul mouthed and inflaming son of discord and faction, a promoter of the lawless excesses of the multitude." He, too, was not a native of the town but had been drawn there by the desire to study law, but he became the most active of the patriots in opposition to the Stamp Act and other similar measures. From 1774 to 1778 he was a member of the Continental Congress, was present on July 4th and August 2d when independence was voted and the Declaration signed.

Unlike the other two Signers, Samuel Chase was practically a self-made man, but his legal practice and his popularity with the Country Party soon brought him considerable wealth. In 1769 he bought a plot of land at what is now the corner of King George Street and Maryland Avenue, then called Northeast Street, for £100 Sterling, and there erected a house almost square on its foundation but three stories high. The height of the first floor above the ground

THE CHASE HOUSE, BUILT BY SAMUEL CHASE IN 1769
Owned by Edward Lloyd, IV and V, from 1771 to 1826

allows room for a great wine cellar with a barrel vault of brick that runs the full depth of the house. The brick work is especially beautiful, for the very thin layers of mortar add a charming delicacy to the construction. At one side is a story-and-a-half wing of brick which contains a huge fireplace with an opening fully ten feet wide.

It is uncertain whether Samuel Chase ever occupied the house, and it may be that it proved to be on a more ambitious scale than he was able to afford, for in 1771 he sold the entire property to Edward Lloyd for £504 Sterling. The simple exterior of the house is in such contrast with the ornate interior with its elaborate carvings, its solid mahogany doors, its silver latches and hinges, the intricate wood carvings of the dining room, and the stucco-decorated ceiling throughout the first floor that it seems as if the Lloyds, a wealthier family, had themselves completed the interior. Here the most admired feature is the staircase. It ascends from the center of the hall to a landing half way up, where, crowned by a beautifully ovalled Palladian window, it divides and rises on either hand to the second floor. The supporting columns are in the purest Ionic style. Other interior features are similarly well-designed and rich, the key to the pantry to be carried on a silken cord by the mistress being of silver.

The structure is essentially a town house, for it stands close to the street, from which a high flight of steps leads to the front door. The semi-circular opening from the sidewalk is fenced by an ancient wooden fence with many slender palings. The garden and lawns surrounding it are ample but not extensive. Not far behind it and in the same square with it is the Governor Ogle residence.

Edward Lloyd, who purchased the house and occupied it during Revolutionary days, was of much more distinguished lineage than its builder. The Lloyds had been among the first Puritan settlers, the first member of the family having been Edward Lloyd, who in 1650 was named "Commander of the Severn." But when he received large grants of land on the opposite shore of the Chesapeake in 1660, he moved there and built Wye House. The fourth Edward Lloyd was the purchaser of the Chase House. He was conspicuous during the Revolution as a member of the Continental Congress, the Committee of Safety of the Eastern Shore, and the provincial Assembly. During hostilities his home at Wye was burned by predatory British soldiers, but in spite of this in 1783 he was assessed as having 500 ounces of silver plate, 72 tracts of land containing 11,884½ acres, 261 slaves, and 215,000 lbs. of tobacco. In 1792, in spite of his being said to be the largest landholder in the State, he supported the proposal to remove the property qualification for voting, and thus gained additional esteem.

Thus occupied as a town house by Colonel Lloyd in his frequent visits to Annapolis on public and private business, the mansion became in 1809 the Governor's mansion, for his son, also Edward Lloyd, became Governor in that year. In all these years it must have been the scene of much brilliant entertaining of French officers at the close of the Revolution and of all the prominent Marylanders of the time.

In 1847 the house came back into the possession of the Chases and in 1888 was bequeathed to the Episcopal Church of Maryland as a home for aged women. As the benefactress was Mrs. Hester Ann Chase Ridout, connected with both the Chases and the Ridouts, one sees to-day in the house some china bearing the Chase coat of arms, a large clock bequeathed to John Ridout by Governor Sharpe, and the latter's sword and punch bowl.

CHAPTER VIII

A GLANCE AT ANNAPOLIS BEFORE THE REVOLUTION

THOUGH we have taken a glance at the principal inhabitants of Annapolis in Colonial days, both Tories and patriots, we have hardly secured an adequate picture of the landmarks of the town or all its citizens worthy of mention. Had a visitor in 1775 climbed to the roof of the State House which still stands, built in the years following 1772 in Governor Eden's time except for the dome, which was not added till several years later, he would have looked down upon the city almost enclosed by the Severn and by Dorsey's Creek to the north and Spa Creek to the south. Its streets would lie about as to-day, stretching out from the State House and St. Anne's like spokes from a hub of a wheel and bearing still familiar names of Duke of Gloucester, King George, Prince George, Cornhill, Fleet, Church, Conduit, West, South, North, Northwest, and Hanover.

To the north from the point of vantage just mentioned the eye would probably first rest on the unroofed and falling walls of "Bladen's Folly," hard by the sturdy trunk and towering branches of the huge poplar tree around which patriotic meetings were already being held to protest against the oppression of Parliament. A little nearer would be seen the Bordley House at the foot of the State House hill. This house was probably built by Thomas Bordley just before his death in 1727, but descended to his son, Stephen Bordley, another lawyer who found Annapolis a favorable place for wealth and reputation by conducting the litigation which was so frequent in colonial Maryland. Stephen Bordley had been educated in England during a stay of ten years, including several years of study at the Temple. When he returned to his native town in 1733 he brought back with him the cultivated tastes of the English gentleman. Beautiful furniture, massive silver plate, and the largest library in Annapolis displayed the distinction of this well-to-do, life-long bachelor. The best wigs to be procured in London were ordered for his appearances in court, and his extant letter books contain mentions of the finest linen and the best cambric being sent for from England.

Bordley was, as might be expected, something of a connoisseur in regard to wines, and we find him writing to his agents, Hill & Co., to order "a pipe of your best Madeira, cost what it will; as I do not stint you in price, I hope you will not slight me in the wine." And writing to his friend James Tilghman, he remarks, "My Burgundy is almost out; but I shall keep some of that as well as of champagne till the Provincial Court, when I hope we shall share it together." It has already been said that in true English style he died of the gout at the early age of fifty-five.

His mansion, now called the Randall House and situated well back from the street in a picturesque garden plot, is the larger of the two brick structures there. Its facade was originally set with lofty columns which extended from the floor of the porch to the eaves of the roof in the general style of Mount Vernon, but these were long ago removed. What remains is, however, still impressive and shows taste and training on the part of the unknown architect. The library is noteworthy. Placed in a sort of connecting passage from the main house to the north wing, it has a surprisingly lofty effect, due to its floor being sunk several feet below the level of the rest of the house and its walls extending clear to the roof

This was also the Annapolis home of John Beale Bordley, a younger half brother. He also was educated in London and himself sent his sons to be similarly trained. Already comfortably wealthy, he married into a family of wealth, the Chews, and then left Annapolis to accept the most lucrative office in the colony, the Prothonotaryship of Baltimore County. After thirteen years of this position he was bequeathed a very valuable estate across the Chesapeake, and moved to the Eastern Shore. Though he lived here most of the rest of his days, he made frequent visits to Annapolis and occupied the old family mansion on such occasions.

With all this wealth and aristocratic mode of living, as well as his membership in the Governor's Council and his incumbency of such offices as Judge of Admiralty, Beale Bordley was a patriot; when the Stamp Act was passed he gave up his office, stopped raising tobacco, and engaged in the cultivation of wheat, which he felt would do the country greater benefit. Later he even established a brewery on his estate to avoid paying taxes on imported liquors, and during the Revolution he started the manufacture of salt to furnish this necessity. After the Revolution he spent some years in Philadelphia, where his scientific interest in agriculture—an interest he shared with such progressive men as Washington—resulted in his publishing several books on husbandry and in his founding an agricultural society which is said to have been the first in the United States.

Had our Revolutionary visitor looked a little farther along down Northeast Street he would have seen just opposite the imposing Chase-Lloyd mansion another fine brick house laid out in the usual Colonial style, a main building two and a half stories high and a wing of less height placed on each side. Built in 1774 its wings are said to have been due to the desire of Edward Lloyd, owner of the Chase House, for an unobstructed view of the harbor. To secure this he offered to pay the expense of wings to avoid having a third story placed on the new house, which is usually known as the Harwood House. The fact that the foundation walls are five feet thick lends probability to the tradition that this change came only after the building had been planned for three full stories.

The builder was Matthias Hammond, another Annapolis lawyer who, like Samuel Chase, was a leader of the popular party before the Revolution, and who took a leading part in the agitation for the burning of the *Peggy Stewart,* the Maryland counterpart of the Boston Tea Party. The tradition is that he erected the house for his prospective bride and furnished it in an elaborate fashion but that the wedding never occurred and Matthias Hammond remained a bachelor all of his days.

The architectural style of the house is ornate but the beautiful gable and cornice across the front and the elaborate woodwork about the front entrance will delight the artist. The interior carvings on the mantelpiece, the window shutters, the door frames, and the doors themselves, all in arabesque, are probably the finest specimens of that sort of design in Maryland. On the second floor is a spacious ballroom twenty-seven feet long and nineteen feet wide.

The house seems to have had no other distinguished occupants during its early years, though the Hammonds were an old and prominent family. In 1810 the house was bought by Ninian Pinkney, whose son, William Pinkney, a Bishop of the Episcopal Church in Maryland, was born here. In 1811 it was sold to a relative of Samuel Chase, from whom it descended to the Harwood family.

Between the Harwood House and the Severn the sightseer of 1775 would notice the square red brick house of Anthony Stewart, successful merchant and strong Tory, situated on Hanover Street, just beyond the brick rectory of St. Anne's where the rector would find himself in a neighborhood almost entirely Tory, for beyond him and nearer the Severn were the large brick dwellings of the Governor and of the Dulanys. From their residences with their well-kept gardens the eye would wander to the harbor with its numerous ships loading the huge hogsheads of tobacco with the help of many singing negroes, and from there continue to the shores of Spa Creek. Here besides the Ridout, Carroll, and Scott houses already mentioned would be seen the lofty chimneys of the block of three houses just beyond the first mentioned and built to be used later by the three children of John Ridout.

A little nearer and slightly closer to the water, on Green Street, where the public school buildings now stand, was the home of Charles Carroll, the Barrister, as he is known to distinguish him from the other two of the same name. A distant relative of the Signer's, he was almost as distinguished and achieved in the State a less prominent, but fully as important, place in history. His father had achieved wealth through several lucrative offices in the colony, and his mother's portrait, perhaps by Sir Godfrey Kneller, attests the distinction of his family. He himself had been a student at Eton, Cambridge, and the Middle Temple, and as soon as he returned to Annapolis in 1746 achieved a reputation as a lawyer, speaker and writer. The fact that he was a Protestant and had always connected himself with the party opposed to the Governor and in favor of the interests of the commercial classes and the smaller land-owners made his career easier. When the Revolution came he assumed a prominent place in all events. He was a member of the Committee of Correspondence, wrote the Declaration of Right issued by the Assembly one day earlier than the Declaration of Independence but breathing the same sentiments, and he was influential in the formation of the new State government. The imposing tomb of the family in St. Anne's churchyard indicates the distinguished place intellectually and socially which he occupied.

Nearer the State House and upon Duke of Gloucester Street would be seen the brick walls of the Assembly Rooms, a distinctive feature of Annapolis, and a characteristic indication of the social life of the town. This had been built in 1764 from the proceeds of a lottery for the accommodation of the society of the city in giving balls, dinners, and other entertainments. Here Washington, as the tablet on the wall attests, danced with the beautiful Mary McCubbin, whose husband was of a family of Annapolis merchants, she the sister of Charles Carroll, the Barrister. Other survivors from Colonial times which remain in this southern and western section of the town are the low lying house on Charles Street, where Jonas Green had his home and printing office, and the Acton estate across an inlet of Spa Creek, where Philip Hammond had built a brick mansion, named for Richard Acton, one of the very earliest inhabitants of the town.

The vicinity about the State House now demands attention. Close to the building on the east side would be found the square structure of the Armory, also used for balls, and on the other side the building for King William's School. In front of the State House would be found a space for a market, while on Church Street, now Main Street, would be seen the principal taverns of the time, the Coffee House and Mann's Tavern, where Washington generally lodged when not entertained by some of his numerous friends.

Behind the State House and in a circle all its own, would have been seen the ruins of St. Anne's. In 1774 the old church, which presented a very dilapidated appearance, had been torn down to erect a better structure, money for which had been secured from the Assembly. But the coming on of the Revolution and the disorganization of the government that preceded it prevented its completion for eighteen years and obliged the congregation that remained to worship in the theater. But around the church would be seen the graves of the most distinguished dead of the town, Amos Garrett, its first mayor, and of many members of the Carroll, Hammond, and Ridgely families. Beyond the site of the church to the west would appear the brick theater erected in 1771 and McCloud's and Hunter's taverns facing each other across the rude street. To the north of the church and across what is now College Avenue but was then called Tabernacle Street, lay Bloomsbury Square, a section where houses of tradesmen and humbler individuals had been located since the early days of the settlement.

CHAPTER IX

STAMP ACT RIOTS AND THE *PEGGY STEWART* TEA PARTY

IN all the colonies before the Revolution disputes between the Governor and the popular assemblies were common, and their existence in Maryland occasions no special comment. But here the Governor was appointed by the Proprietary and was obliged to pursue toward the representatives of the people the selfish and narrow-minded policies which he prescribed so frequently. The habit of opposition was therefore deeply ingrained; a typical case was the difficulties Governor Sharpe encountered in securing grants of money from the Colonial treasury to protect the western frontier from the very real danger of Indian and French attack. The Assembly voted the money but imposed the condition that the lands of the Proprietary should be taxed like other property. But this Lord Baltimore maintained was illegal, since the Assembly years before had, in return for certain concessions, exempted these lands from such taxes. He therefore stubbornly refused to allow the Governor to sign the bill, and little money was secured for defense.

So stupid was this attitude that even Governor Sharpe in his private correspondence deprecated the very action he was obliged to take, and the natural result was to increase the strength of the popular, or country, party. To the "Court Party" adhered the office holders, the clergy, and many of the larger merchants, while the popular party was distinguished by the number of lawyers who directed its activities and by the support of the smaller land holders. To it also belonged the chief Catholic land-owners, since now that the Baltimore family had become Protestant—a change that occurred in 1715—they found themselves discriminated against by the aristocratic party and subjected to double taxation when money was urgently needed. Their chief hopes for redress seemed to them to lie in the more democratic group, at least in the party not then in power.

Although the British Government tried to punish the colonials for their niggardly support of the French wars by quartering at one time five companies of troops in Annapolis, the first real note of Revolutionary feeling was struck when the Stamp Act was passed in 1765. Probably at no time later were the Americans so united in opposition to Parliament and the Ministry. Governor Sharpe wrote home:

"What lengths the people, now they have once begun, may go, is not easy to say, but as the inhabitants of all the colonies with regard to the Stamp Act Law seem to act as it were in concert, it will not I think be possible without a considerable military force in each colony to let it have its effect."

In Annapolis the action in concert was a vote by both houses of the Legislature to appropriate money to send delegates to New York to a congress which should frame a common protest from all the colonies. But popular feeling did not stop at this measure. On August 27th when Annapolitans heard of the appointment of Zachariah Hood, a merchant of the town, as distributor of stamped paper, a mob paraded through the streets with an effigy of Hood riding in a cart like a felon to the gallows and hold-

Stamp Act Riots

ing several sheets of the obnoxious stamped paper before its face. With the bells tolling, the crowd proceeded to the town whipping-post and pillory and gave the dummy figure a lashing. They then hung it on the gallows and burned it over a lighted tar barrel.

When Hood, who was on his way from London, arrived, an angry mob tried to prevent his landing, and one member of the crowd, Thomas McNeir, had his thigh broken in the scuffle—the first American, it is said, injured in the patriot cause. A little later a crowd of three or four hundred assembled and pulled down a building where Hood intended to store the goods he brought back and perhaps the stamped paper. All this frightened Hood so much that he tried to resign his commission and when Governor Sharpe would not accept it fled to New York.

But the Sons of Liberty, an organization of the patriots, even here pursued him. Finding him in a village on Long Island, they gathered about the house and demanded that he sign an abject resignation and apology and confirm it by oath before a magistrate. After several hours of delay, Hood gave in to the New Yorkers, and escorted by nearly a hundred patriots proceeded to Flushing, where before a magistrate he attested the genuineness of his resignation. His signed declaration stated that he resigned "with the utmost cheerfulness and willingness." Later he returned to Annapolis and was not molested in re-establishing his business. Compensation was even voted to the owner of the house destroyed and to the mechanic whose tools there had disappeared.

As the printers and stationers expected their business to be ruined by the refusal of the people to buy stamped paper, they were loudest in their opposition. The *Maryland Gazette* appeared in deep mourning and announced that it would cease publication before it would submit. This was the general resolution, and even the judges of the courts and the officials of the Land Office, upon the demand of the Sons of Liberty, decided to carry on their work without obeying the law. When, on April 5th of the next year, the news came of the repeal of the Act, there was a general celebration.

Probably the most powerful and influential agitation against the Stamp Act came from

Daniel Dulany, the Younger, an eminent lawyer closely associated with the Court Party and at this very time Secretary of the Province and a member of the Governor's Council. His pamphlet, "Considerations on the Propriety of Imposing Taxes in the British Colonies for the Purpose of Raising a Revenue by Act of Parliament," was a thoroughly scholarly and legal argument against the very foundations of the Stamp Act and the later right of taxation which Parliament asserted.

The basic contention of the pamphlet—the most noteworthy product of the Annapolis press—was that while Parliament and the Crown might impose restrictions on the trade of the colonies with the mother country, other colonies, or foreign nations, and might even tax such transactions, any internal taxation except that imposed by the colonial Assemblies was contrary to British Constitutional law and the special charters granted the various colonies. The pamphlet was also published and read in England. Pitt exhibited the pamphlet in the House of Commons in his denunciation of the Act and incorporated many of its arguments in his speeches. So grateful were the Marylanders for Pitt's assistance that when the news of repeal came the Assembly voted to erect a marble statue of their English champion and to place a portrait of Lord Camden, who had been their defender in the House of Lords, in the provincial court room. It is sad to relate that these resolutions were, however, never executed.

When in 1767 the Townshend Acts were passed, the flame of opposition rose anew. Dickinson's "Letters of a Pennsylvania Farmer" were reprinted in the *Gazette,* and the public, more sensitive than ever to any direct taxation, again resolved to nullify the hated measure. In 1768 representatives of the Colonies met in Boston and organized a non-importation movement. By 1769 Maryland had joined the association and even the merchants in Annapolis who would be most affected were foremost in consolidating sentiment against bringing in goods with the tax. Committees for the various counties were appointed to see that no ship came in with goods that were to be boycotted. In the case of the *"Good Intent"* in 1770, the Committee for Anne Arundel decided that the cargo must go back or at least not be landed. Governor Eden protested, and asserted that to send the brig back would make it "liable to be seized in the first British port she enters for carrying back Indian goods and other things contrary to the conditions of the bonds given on shipping them; liable also to action on every bill of lading given by the captain, who could not act otherwise than he has done any more than the merchants themselves."

As these events furnished the bulk of the argument by which the patriots of 1775 were to support their cause, so a minor dispute between the Assembly and the Governor over the right to fix the fees of the various colonial officials, especially in the courts and the Land Office, brought forth the men who were to be the chief patriot leaders. This time Daniel Dulany, the author of the "Considerations," took the side of the Governor while Charles Carroll of Carrollton for the first time appeared as a champion of the people. In the *Gazette* there appeared a dialogue between "First Citizen" and "Second Citizen" in which the arguments and sincerity of the popular party were impugned. Carroll immediately wrote a reply and assumed the designation, "First Citizen," which had been given his side. Thereupon, Dulany, who seems well known as the author of the original dialogue, came to the defense of his •party under the name of "Antilon," probably a Spanish word for an astringent plaster which draws the poison from a wound.

The debate shows the high level of legal and literary discussion then in vogue among the educated men of the time. To the modern mind it is too subtle, too personal, and too long drawn out to be effective or interesting. Latin and legal quotations abound; Dulany taunts his opponent with being a citizen without a vote— a reference to Carroll's disfranchisement as a Catholic—and Carroll retorts by denouncing Dulany's lucrative connections and offices. The local political result was the election in May, 1773, of two patriot representatives from Annapolis, William Paca and Matthias Hammond, and the defeat of the candidate of the Court Party, Anthony Stewart, the later victim of popular wrath in the controversy over tea. And in a controversy over the payment of taxes for the benefit of the Established Church, which was

Stamp Act Riots 145

another feature of this controversy, Samuel Chase also showed himself as a prominent agitator. Thus the chief leaders of two years later were foreshadowed.

Before the end of 1773, however, the attention of the people was turned from local to more general matters. On account of the non-importation agreements, imperfectly observed as they were, there had been a heavy reduction in imports, and a surplus stock of tea accumulating in England was embarrassing the East India Company. The effort to dispose of this tea in 1773 and 1774 in America at prices lower than were asked in England but with the obnoxious tax included started a train of events which led straight to the Revolution.

In Boston, on the 28th of November, 1773, the Boston Tea Party occurred. When the next March Parliament met it passed the Boston Port Bill in retaliation and closed the port to commerce, all soon followed by other punitive measures. This quickly aroused the other colonies to resolutions of sympathy and to organizations for the relief of Boston. Writing from Annapolis in May, 1774, Eddis, loyalist though he is, says: "All America is in a flame: I hear strange language every day. The colonists are ripe for any measure that will tend to the preservation of what they call their natural liberty," and later, "The spirit of opposition to ministerial measures appears to blaze steadily and equally in every part of British America and unless some speedy alteration takes place in the political system, the consequences must inevitably be dreadful."

On the 25th of May an Annapolis meeting adopted resolutions of sympathy with Boston and appointed a committee of correspondence to act with other parts of the colony and with other colonies. On the 4th of June the inhabitants of Anne Arundel met at Annapolis and adopted a non-importation agreement. They even urged lawyers not to conduct suits against colonists for debts unpaid because of this, but there was considerable opposition to this particular provision.

During this summer, while Governor Eden, who had succeeded Sharpe in 1769, was absent in England, the real independence of Maryland may be said to have begun. The committees which saw to it that the non-importation agreement was observed gradually took over the supervision of other matters in the colony. They even later directed the forming of a colonial militia and the care of the munitions of war then on hand and passed resolutions in regard to the work of courts and record offices which were obeyed as if laws. Governor Eden returned in November and remained in Annapolis till 1776, but, though he occupied the Governor's Mansion, he had hardly any influence over events. As Eddis wrote his friend in England, "Government is now almost totally annihilated, and power transferred to the multitude."

While the Governor was still absent, in October, 1774, occurred the *Peggy Stewart* Tea Party, as the affair is now named by patriotic Marylanders, who often feel some resentment at the average American's familiarity with the Boston Tea Party and his total ignorance of what to them seems a finer exhibition of American spirit in Annapolis less than a year later. In Boston there was secrecy and disguise and a mere dumping of the tea overboard; in Annapolis the disposition of the tea was discussed and decided upon openly in popular assembly, and the owners of the tea and of the vessel in which it had arrived were persuaded to apologize for their unpatriotic acts and destroy in one spectacular conflagration both vessel and detested cargo.

On the 14th of May, 1774, Messrs. Williams & Company, merchants of Annapolis, had ordered from London 2320 lbs. of tea. This was before the non-importation agreements had been put into force. On July 23d the tea left London in the brig *Peggy Stewart,* owned by Anthony Stewart and named for his daughter. In the summer the agitation against importation became stronger and this produced a situation that presaged trouble. This was realized as soon as the brig arrived in the harbor of Annapolis on the 14th of October. Handbills were immediately circulated calling for a meeting of the citizens of the city and county on the following Wednesday to determine what should be done about the tea. The prime mover in this seems to have been Matthias Hammond, who was a member of the committee of correspondence. In the meantime the committee itself had met because of information which reached it that at ten o'clock that

*From an etching by E. P. Metour, by permission of
E. H. Curlander, Art Dealer, Baltimore*

THE STATE HOUSE FROM NORTH STREET

morning the ship and cargo had been entered at the custom house and the duty on the tea paid by Anthony Stewart. The committee therefore called a meeting of the people at five o'clock that afternoon and ordered the captain of the brig, the owner of the vessel, the owners of the tea, and the deputy-collector of the port to attend.

When the citizens assembled they were informed by the Williams firm that it left the matter in the hands of the Committee to decide the disposal of the tea. Either storing it in Annapolis or reshipping it to London, the West Indies, or elsewhere would be agreeable to them. They further defended themselves by asserting that they had not intended to land the tea until its disposition had been decided by the Committee. The master of the brig, Captain Jackson, stated that the tea had been placed in the vessel in London without his knowledge. And Anthony Stewart explained that his action was due entirely to motives of humanity in as much as the ship had on board a crew of six men and also fifty-three indentured servants. They must be landed at once after their long sea voyage and also because of the leaky condition of the ship.

No passenger or part of the cargo could be brought ashore till the vessel had been entered at the custom house and all the cargo declared and the duties paid or surety given for their payment.

Only one fact, however, was brought out that was at all favorable to the offenders. That was that the tea was still on the vessel. When therefore the committee and the meeting voted whether the tea should be landed there was a unanimous "no." And a committee was appointed to supervise the unloading of the rest of the cargo and see that the tea should remain on board. A guard was even placed on the brig to make sure of this.

Whereas it is probable that Stewart as the owner of the brig but not of the tea would have escaped serious punishment for his part, the fact that he had arranged to pay the tax inflamed popular sentiment against him, and he and the Williams brothers who composed the firm of Williams & Company were required to read and sign the following abject letter of apology:

"We, James Williams, Joseph Williams, and Anthony Stewart," it read, "do severally acknowledge that we have committed a most daring insult and act of the most pernicious tendency to the liberties of America; we, the said Williams, in importing the tea, and said Stewart in paying the duty thereon; and thereby deservedly incurred the displeasure of the people now convened, and all others interested in the preservation of the constitutional rights and liberties of North America; do ask pardon for the same; and we solemnly declare for the future, that we never will infringe any resolution framed by the people for the salvation of their rights, nor will we do any act that may be injurious to the liberties of the people; and to show our desire of living in amity with the friends to America, we do request this meeting or as many as may choose to attend, to be present at any place where the people shall appoint, and we will there commit to the flames or otherwise destroy as the people may choose, the detestable article which has been the cause of this, our misconduct.

   (Signed) ANTHONY STEWART,
         JOSEPH WILLIAMS,
         JAMES WILLIAMS."

Eddis, who was an eye-witness of the scene, says, "Though he (Anthony Stewart) publicly read his recantation, expressed in the most submissive and penitential terms, there were frantic zealots among the multitude who warmly proposed the American discipline of tarring and feathering."[1]

In spite of this suggestion of personal violence, and of others such as that Stewart should be required to burn the ship and build another, to be named "Wilkes and Liberty,"—alluding to the help John Wilkes had given the American cause,—the meeting definitely voted not to have the vessel destroyed. But the feeling was so strong against Stewart that finally he decided, on the urging apparently of some of the patriot leaders, of whom Charles Carroll of Carrollton is said to have been the most influential, to burn the ship himself. So, on this very day, the 19th, accompanied by a number of the patriots, he sailed the brig across the harbor till she grounded on Windmill Point, now a part of the level space between Bancroft Hall and the harbor line, left the sails set, and with his own hand set

[1] Eddis, "Letters from America," p. 182.

fire to the vessel and its cargo of tea. It is said that his wife and daughter were able to witness the burning from the windows of their home, which has since become, curiously enough, a shrine for patriotic Marylanders.

Stewart remained in Annapolis after this, but eventually found himself *persona non grata* to the growing patriotic feeling, was hanged or burned in effigy in various places, and obliged to leave his wife and family and go to England. There he entered claim for compensation for the loss of his vessel. Thomas C. Williams, of the Williams firm, who had supervised the shipping of the tea from London, arrived in New York the very day the people there heard of the entry of the tea. As a result he had to flee for his life and conceal himself in the woods, as he states in his affidavit. Then a price was set on his head and he was later obliged to escape from Philadelphia by night and abandon all his property and business prospects. He seems, though, to have finally reached Annapolis, for a statement in the *Maryland Gazette* of January 12, 1775, makes humble apologies for his part in the matter and begs leave to live in the town.

CHAPTER X

OPENING THE REVOLUTION—A CONTEST IN COURTESY

JUST as the affair of the *Peggy Stewart* shows a higher level of popular action against what the people regarded as oppression than is often emphasized by traditional accounts, in that the action taken was open and deliberate rather than the result of mob psychology, so in the events that preceded the total destruction of British rule in Maryland there is seen a mutual consideration for the personal feelings of both Royalist and patriot which is frequently passed over and forgotten. Vigorous as the action of the patriots of Annapolis and the colony was it did not attempt to precipitate matters but moved ahead in a dignified, deliberate fashion which is evidence of strength and deep conviction of the rightness of its course.

Even before the burning of Anthony Stewart's brig, the Continental Congress had assembled in Philadelphia,—its first meeting due largely to the suggestion of the Maryland Convention, as the popular assembly was then called, of June 22-25, 1774. At the first meeting two of the Maryland delegates were from Annapolis, William Paca and Samuel Chase. When these delegates reported to their electors in November, the Convention approved their actions and unanimously agreed to the scheme of non-importation recommended by Congress. It ordered that all balls be discontinued, that the people should be urged not to kill lambs but to raise them for the wool, to promote the manufacture of woolens, to plant hemp, flax, and cotton, and to export no flax seed. It even voted to organize militia companies, explaining with sly humor "that such a militia will relieve our mother country from any expenses in our protection and defense; will obviate the pretense of a necessity for taxing us on that account, and render it unnecessary to keep any standing army (ever dangerous to liberty) in this province." In Annapolis three such companies were recruited, and, as it was said, "gentlemen of the first fortune are common soldiers."

By a resolution adopted in January, 1775, at a meeting in Annapolis of the inhabitants of the county, "Every inhabitant who shall refuse to contribute before the 1st day of February next to the purchase of arms and ammunition for the use of this county is, and ought to be, esteemed an enemy to America, and shall have his name published in the *Gazette*." When the news of the engagement at Lexington reached the city on April 28th, there was great excitement, and the direction of the Continental Congress that it was "night and day to be forwarded, until it had penetrated the farthest recesses of the colonies" was instantly obeyed.

And although the Convention of 1775 had affirmed that a reconciliation with Great Britain was "an event we most ardently wish may soon take place," by June of 1776 popular feeling had so developed, even among the leaders, that the previous instructions to the delegates in Congress were repealed and the delegates allowed to concur with the ideas of the majority. On July 3d the Convention in Annapolis adopted what may well be called Maryland's own Declaration of Independence. Its conclusion reads, as may be seen from the original copy preserved against further damage in the Senate Chamber of the State House:

"Compelled by dire necessity, either to surrender our properties, liberties, and lives into the hands of a British king and parliament, or to use such means as will most probably secure to us and our posterity those invaluable blessings,—

"*We, the Delegates of Maryland,* in convention assembled, do declare that the king of Great Britain has violated his compact with his people, and that they owe no allegiance to him; we have therefore thought it just and necessary to empower our deputies in Congress to join with a majority of the United Colonies in declaring them free and independent States, in framing such further confederation between them, in making foreign alliances, and in adopting such other measures as shall be judged necessary for the preservation of their liberties: provided the sole and exclusive rights of regulating the internal polity and government of this colony be reserved for the people thereof. We have also thought proper to call a new convention for the purpose of establishing a government in this colony. No ambitious views, no desire for independence, induced the people of Maryland to form a union with the other colonies. To procure an exemption from parliamentary taxation, and to continue to the legislatures of these colonies the sole and exclusive right of regulating their internal polity, was our original and only motive. To maintain inviolate our liberties, and to transmit them unimpaired to posterity, was our duty and first wish; our next to continue connected with, and dependent on, Great Britain. For the truth of these assertions we appeal to that Almighty Being who is emphatically styled the Searcher of hearts, and from whose omniscience nothing is concealed. Relying on His divine protection and affiance, and trusting to the justice of our cause, we exhort and conjure every virtuous citizen to join cordially in the defense of our common rights, and in maintenance of the freedom of this and her sister colonies."

With this support it was natural for the three Maryland delegates who were present in Philadelphia on July 4th—of whom William Paca from Annapolis was one—to cast the vote of

Maryland in favor of the Declaration of Independence. In Annapolis the Declaration was published in the *Maryland Gazette* of July 11th, and on August 2d when the members of Congress inscribed their names to the engrossed copy three Annapolitan signatures appeared, those of William Paca, Samuel Chase, and Charles Carroll of Carrollton.

Vigorous as such steps were in the actual work of achieving independence, the Maryland Convention and the Committee of Correspondence which had its headquarters in Annapolis displayed a rarer quality—a fine sense of courtesy and consideration for the opposite party and especially for Sir Robert Eden, who was placed in a position even more difficult than the patriots themselves. Thoroughly loyal to the British government and never truckling merely to popular feeling or considerations of personal safety or advantage, he nevertheless appreciated the feelings of the colonists and sought in every way to prevent actual violence or bloodshed and secure an eventual reconciliation by mutual understanding and concession. And in the whole course of events the leaders of the patriotic party and Eden prevented any break in this record of courtesy except when interfered with by outsiders.

During Governor Eden's absence in England in 1774 the control of affairs had gradually drifted into the hands of the Committee of Correspondence, and when he returned he saw that any attempt to reassert his authority would be unsuccessful and result only in further trouble. The arrival of troops would only produce additional disturbance. Therefore in the spring of 1775, when General Gage in Boston and Lord Dunmore in Virginia were creating ill-feeling by seizing the arms and powder of the colonists, Eden responded favorably to a demand of the Convention that the stores should be given into its charge for fear of an attempt of a ship of war to capture them. But he asked and secured the concession that the colonels of militia to whom these stores should be delivered should be the officers appointed by him before his departure for England in the previous year. And he secured the approval of the British Colonial Office to his action.

The Convention appreciated the moderation

of the Governor and when it voted that all persons should sign the Articles of Association or leave the colony, it exempted the Governor and the members of his household. And it construed this liberally, for we find the Governor inviting Eddis to become a member of his household just for the purpose of saving himself from expulsion. When he considered publishing a proclamation urging the people to avoid any act of rebellion or excess, the Council of Safety, which was authorized to act for the Convention during the intervals between sessions, wrote him in opposition but mentioned sympathetically his delicate situation as one "having duties both to England and to Maryland," and it assured him that they were not seeking independence.

In order to assure the Governor in case a war vessel should anchor in the harbor, a public meeting voted they would supply it with necessities at a reasonable price and would avoid any cause of contention with the officers or crew. And as late as January, 1776, Eddis writes that Governor Eden continued to receive "every external mark of attention and respect; while the steady propriety of his conduct in many trying exigencies reflects the utmost credit on his moderation and understanding."

Eden's genuine wish for reconciliation and his candor are well illustrated by his inviting the chief patriots to a dinner at his house. Apparently the idea originated with Daniel of St. Thomas Jenifer, a member of the Governor's Council but a sympathizer with the contentions of the popular party. When the chief leaders of the opposition had to decline an invitation to dinner at Jenifer's house in Southern Maryland, where the Governor was spending Christmas, the Governor himself issued an invitation through Barrister Carroll, but when those invited feared that meeting at the Governor's board might place them in an embarrassing situation, Carroll himself gathered the Governor and the patriots around his own table. Among these were Matthew Tilghman, Thomas Johnson, James Hollyday, Thomas Stone, and Samuel Chase. The candor of both sides showed the respect each had for the other.

This is illustrated by the story that at one point the Governor said, "It is understood in England that the Congress are about forming a treaty with France." At first no one wished to answer, but finally Thomas Johnson, the Marylander who had nominated Washington for commander-in-chief and who became the first Governor under independence, replied, "Well, sir, we will candidly acknowledge that overtures have been made to France, but they are not yet accepted." "Now, sir," Johnson continued, "we understand that the King, your master, is about subsidizing a large body of Hessians to join his forces to come over to cut our throats." To this the Governor replied with equal candor that he believed the report was true.

The delicate, almost impossible, situation of having two sovereign powers functioning at the same time in the province was saved only by the most careful management and consideration in the various crises that occurred. One was in March, 1776, when the British armed ship *Otter* appeared off the mouth of the Severn. The patriots feared an attack on the town, but Eden moved energetically to avert such a result. Applying—a fact that shows his impotence but also his peaceful policy—to the Council of Safety for a flag of truce, he sent his friend William

Eddis to the commander of the sloop to assure him of the moderation of the inhabitants, their aversion to independence, and their decent treatment of the Governor. In reply the British officer stated that he had come only to seize a privateer in Baltimore and to buy flour for the navy, for which he would pay market prices. He also explained the burning of a small patriot vessel off the Severn as the work of a midshipman acting without orders.

A curious turn of events then ensued. The captain of the *Otter* applied to the Governor for permission to buy provisions and for authority to commandeer the flour and bread on a small New England sloop then lying in the river. Eden turned the letter over to the Council of Safety, which said that it would have granted the favor had the *Otter* not burned the schooner in the bay. On that account they refused the request and put a guard on the New England sloop to prevent its capture. Yet in refusing, the Council acknowledged the wisdom of Eden's course in the following words: "We are much obliged to your Excellency for the pains you have taken to preserve the peace of this province

Opening the Revolution   165

and beg that you will still exert your endeavors for the restoration of those happy days that we enjoyed under a constitutional dependence on the mother country."[1]

The refusal did not bring on hostile action by the commander of the *Otter*. Instead he had recourse to diplomacy; he sent ashore under a flag of truce some prisoners he had taken, all of whom testified that they had been kindly treated. Immediately the Council of Safety could not bear to be outdone in courtesy. "In return," the record states, "it was thought proper to compliment the officer with two quarters of beef." With this the *Otter* sailed away without firing a gun. It is even probable that the diplomacy of the ship's captain was suggested to him by Eden himself.

So moderate had been the tone of the Council of Safety, whose membership was nearly one-half made up of inhabitants of Annapolis, that the patriots of Baltimore and the more radical group in Virginia began to suspect their loyalty. Thus when letters from England to Governor Eden were intercepted and when read were

[1] "Maryland Archives," Vol. XI, p. 233.

thought to indicate that he had been sending over a list of patriots upon whom extreme punishment should be inflicted, and that he was asking, and was to secure, an armed expedition against the Middle and Southern colonies, the military commander in Virginia, Major-General Charles Lee, sent the letters to the patriot committee in Baltimore and entirely ignored the Council in Annapolis. They were in his words "timorous and inactive" and "afraid to execute the duties of their stations." He therefore urged the patriots of Baltimore to act on their own initiative and order the commander of the troops in the capital city to arrest the Governor.

Instead of doing this, however, Purviance, the Baltimore chairman, sent the letters to the Council, and they, after considering them, sent Charles Carroll, the Barrister, John Hall and William Paca to Eden for an explanation. The Governor assured them that he had said nothing unfriendly to the province, had asked for no troops, and had traduced the characters of no individuals. As, however, the Governor could not produce the original letter, they asked, as they had been instructed, for his parole that he

DRYING SAILS IN MARKET SLIP

From an etching by E. P. Metour, by permission of E. H. Curlander, Art Dealer, Baltimore

would not leave the province before the assembling of the Convention on May 27th. When the Governor demurred at this he was given one day in which to consider his answer.

Before this time expired events had moved fast. The Continental Congress had read the letters and had voted to ask the Maryland Council to seize Eden and to send all his papers to Philadelphia. Although the Maryland delegates protested against this interference, it was to no avail. Meantime the Baltimore Committee had fitted out an armed boat and sent it to Annapolis to seize the Governor and bring him to Baltimore without consulting any one. When it arrived the situation was unfavorable and no attempt was made. The Governor's barge did, however, come along and was captured with some bottles of porter and claret which the captors soon consumed as spoils of war. As the commander of the armed force had not been told the secrecy of the scheme, he ingenuously revealed it to Barrister Carroll, one of the members of the Council, and he at once informed him that no such orders had been issued by the

Council and ordered him to return at once to Baltimore.

By the next noon Eden had returned an answer to the Council in a manly and sensible letter, addressed to the committee which had waited on him. It read as follows:

"Annapolis, 17th April 1776
"Gentlemen:

"However unwelcome might be your errand, your polite behavior to me yesterday merits my acknowledgments. And on mature consideration of the proposal you made to me, I find it incumbent on me to tell you that I will not accord to it, nor can I, whilst I act in any degree as Governor of this province, give my parole to walk about in it a prisoner at large under any obligations whatever. The necessity must be obvious of my ceasing to act as Governor should I become a prisoner, neither will I voluntarily give you any satisfaction on that head further than that I had, and have, no intention during these times of leaving the province whilst my continuing here can in my own opinion tend to preserve its tranquillity.

"My resolution was, as the letters you have of

Opening the Revolution 169

mine show, to continue here whilst I could serve the province; nor shall the indignity now offered to me alter it. I shall persevere in my line of duty by what I think the rule of right, but not without some chagrin at knowing myself unmeritedly the object of suspicion, although I have the satisfaction to think that a considerable part of the most respectable persons in the province entertain a very different opinion of me than is to be inferred from your proposed arrest.

"May I not challenge you to say to the world if any troops have arrived at, or any hostile measures been proceeded in against, this province from any request of mine or information from me to the Secretary of State? I have above told you my resolution of continuing in my station as long as permitted, or the ostensible form of the established government can contribute to preserve the peace of the province; and I will add one further assurance, in hopes it may be satisfactory to you, that as your Convention is to meet shortly they shall find me here, and willing to continue acting in the same line I have hitherto done, so long as Maryland can reap any peaceful benefits from my service, provided I can have assurances that my peaceful departure shall not be impeded, whenever I find my remaining any longer here unnecessary or that my private affairs at home indispensably demand my return.

"Consistent with my honor and insulted station I cannot add more but that, if made a prisoner, I shall consider myself treated as an enemy, and such a proceeding as a breach of that confidence I have implicitly reposed in you, which I thought my conduct and the public declaration of the Convention justified. I am, gentlemen, with respect,

"Your obedient and humble servant,

"ROBERT EDEN.

"To Charles Carroll, Esq., Barrister, John Hall, Esq., & William Paca, Esq."[1]

The Council answered in a tone that showed they still respected Eden and understood how difficult was his situation. They seemed to apologize for their more radical compatriots in Baltimore and Philadelphia, and they mention again their hope for a speedy reconciliation. They

[1] "Maryland Archives," Vol. XI, pp. 337-8.

Opening the Revolution 171

thank him for assuring them that he will remain as long as he can assist in solving their difficulties or preserving public quiet. If he wishes to leave at any time they promise to do their utmost to remove any obstacle.

The Council then acted on the request of Congress for Eden's arrest. It refused to admit the right of Congress to so order inasmuch as the matter was a domestic one and not subject to outside supervision. They stated that they had known of the intercepted letters before Congress had seen them and that they had taken such action as they considered best. In a letter to the Maryland delegates they go farther and contend that Eden's friendly letters to the British authorities, and the fact that he had not been arrested or the government of the colony formally destroyed, had saved Maryland the horrors of attack and had left open the door of reconciliation. Furthermore, they state that the Convention had given them no authority to overturn the existing government or to arrest the Governor and thus accomplish the same result.[1]

But the courtesies of the occasion were not

[1] "Maryland Archives," Vol. XI, pp. 349-50.

exhausted. On Monday Eden sent for several members of the Council and showed his appreciation of their attitude by giving them his parole not to leave Maryland till the Convention should meet. And this was in spite of the fact that the Council felt obliged to search the Governor's letter files, only to discover there several letters to friends in England in which he had spoken favorably of the colonists.

It is important to notice that when the Convention met on May 6, 1776, it approved the acts of the Council of Safety and severely reprimanded Purviance for his assumption of authority. It even denied the statement of the Continental Congress that it was now time every sort of Royal authority should be suppressed—a demand which plainly meant the expulsion of Eden. But in view of the difficulties of the situation both for themselves and for him, they desire that he shall put the President of the Council in charge of affairs, thus preserving the form of government, and leave the province. In their address to him they almost outdo courtesy in expressing their "favorable sense of his conduct," his efforts to promote the real interests of both countries, and his true representation of their tempers. They express the hope that "when the unhappy disputes which at present prevail are constitutionally accommodated, he may speedily return and re-assume the reins of government."

The committee which carried this address to Governor Eden went even further, apparently without authority but in full confidence that they would be sustained. They proposed that he should give his word not to correspond with the British Government at all, and should under those circumstances continue as Governor and remain in the Governor's Mansion. This was because the committee felt that there was still hope of settlement and that his continuing the old forms of government would assist in securing a peaceful solution. And this was less than six weeks before the Declaration of Independence!

The Governor felt, however, that this would be going too far for a servant of the Crown and therefore agreed to leave as soon as he could make arrangements for a British man-of-war to come for him. The preparations for departure were exceedingly friendly. He called his Council together, and as their last act they issued writs for the election of a new Legislature. On the evening of the 22d of June the British warship *Fowey,* Captain George Montague, arrived in the harbor to receive Governor Eden. Before he embarked he took an affectionate farewell of the Council of Safety and they conducted him to his barge with every token of respect. It looked as though the relations between Governor and people were to end amicably.

But just then fate interfered. Captain Montague had received on board his ship some indentured servants and a deserter from the militia. These he refused to give up on the strength of his orders to furnish refuge to any person "well affected" to the Crown. Even Eden's representations to the commander, at the request of the Council, were ineffectual. When Montague sent in the next morning to know why the Governor's baggage had not been sent on board, he was informed that it was because he had broken his flag of truce. With such mutual recriminations the *Fowey* sailed away, leaving behind the baggage of the Governor and with an ill feeling created which both the Governor and the Coun-

Opening the Revolution 175

cil had labored so hard to prevent. It is characteristic of Eden that after the Revolution he returned to Maryland and lived there until his death in 1784. He died in the home of his friend Dr. Upton Scott and was buried beneath the pulpit of St. Margaret's Church on Severn Heights across from Annapolis. The church was burned many years ago and was never rebuilt on the same spot. But in the rough thicket which now covers the site the lines of the foundation may still be traced, though no clear indication of the spot where Eden lies can be discovered.

Though Governor Eden had left and the whole Royal government had been overturned by the Declaration of Independence, many offices continued as if no change had taken place. Eddis, who was one of the Commissioners of the Loan Office, carried on his work in spite of the fact that in June, 1776, he had refused to give bonds not to communicate with the enemy and had been ordered to leave the province by the first of August. Instead, his family having already returned to England, he simply removed to a secluded spot near Baltimore, Hunting Ridge, and visited Annapolis every other week to supervise his office. Not till April, 1777, was he superseded in his place, and not till June did he leave Annapolis for Hampton Roads, where after much difficulty he reached the British fleet and embarked.

In fact, the Land Office—so gradual was the separation from the old forms of government—still issued patents on the authority of the Lord Proprietary till May 15, 1777, although by that time the colony had been declared independent, a revolutionary Governor and Council elected, and a Constitution framed which recognized neither Lord Baltimore, who made the grant, nor the King from whom the Proprietary derived all his authority. In such gradual, almost halting fashion so characteristic of the practical genius of the English race, as opposed to French logic and Teutonic directness, did Maryland pass from under the British Crown and assume the full manhood of independence.[1]

[1] For much of the material of this chapter I am indebted to B. C. Steiner's "Life and Administration of Governor Eden," in John Hopkins Historical Studies, Series XVI, Nos. 7-8-9.

CHAPTER XI

LAFAYETTE AND ROCHAMBEAU IN ANNAPOLIS, 1781

AS a part of a State in which no real battle was fought during the Revolution—in this Maryland and New Hampshire were alone—Annapolis does not appear in any of the military annals of the war. The mouth of the Severn was fortified, a battery was placed on Windmill Point, several companies of troops were recruited in the town and sailed away for the head of Chesapeake Bay in time to take part in the Brandywine campaign, British warships passed up and down the Chesapeake at intervals, causing fears of an attack which never came, and distinguished generals like Greene and von Steuben passed through the town enchanting the hearts of young men and maidens with their brilliant uniforms and dashing aides-de-camp—but that was all.

The real heyday of military activity in Annapolis did not come until the French troops appeared in 1781. Then regiments of Americans under Lafayette and French soldiers of Rochambeau occupied the town on several occasions, and Washington's own troops from the Northern Army passed down the bay on their way to Yorktown.

First came Lafayette in March, 1781, on his way to Virginia to reinforce the Americans there fighting Benedict Arnold. At the same time a French fleet had sailed from Newport for the Chesapeake to assist the Continental forces, prevent reinforcements reaching Arnold or Cornwallis, and perhaps to accomplish the actual capture of Arnold, the hated traitor and renegade. Lafayette marched his men by land from Washington's headquarters near New York till he reached the Head of Elk on the 9th of March. Here, at the upper end of the Chesapeake, he was supposed to wait till the arrival of the French ships in the Chesapeake guaranteed him safe passage by water to Virginia.

But Lafayette soon saw that the French would be unlikely to render him much assistance, and as he had a little fleet of Continental ships under Commodore Nicholson he moved his men

Lafayette and Rochambeau 179

on to Annapolis by water, effectively protected by his own ships. But from there down he was unwilling to risk attack and accordingly left his forces in the town while he proceeded down the bay in a small boat to find the French fleet and secure convoy.

When, however, Lafayette arrived in Virginia he found no signs of the French and soon learned that the squadron had been forced back to Newport by a British attack. He accordingly followed the instructions he had received from Washington, returned to Annapolis, and re-embarked his men for the Head of Elk for a return north. But when he was ready to leave he found himself blockaded by two British vessels, the *Hope,* of twenty guns, and the *Monk,* of eighteen. The people of Annapolis urged him to hold his troops in their town to safeguard the place, but Lafayette was anxious to be on his way and he did not relish marching by land and crossing the many rivers and inlets between the Severn and the Elk.

What he finally did was to fit out two merchantmen with a few cannon and several hundred volunteers and sail boldly out to meet the enemy. Thereupon the British blockaders moved off and Lafayette brought his troops up the bay without molestation.

By the summer of 1781 the campaign of Yorktown was making Annapolis an important base for troops and supplies. At the end of August and the beginning of September two regiments of Marylanders were organized here and marched off for Virginia. By the first week of the latter month the French fleet under De Grasse had arrived at the entrance of the Chesapeake and closed the bay to British expeditions. French ships of war passed up and down the bay, anchored in the mouth of the Severn, and embarked troops at Annapolis. About the 12th the vanguard of the Franco-American army from the north arrived on its way to Yorktown. On the 18th, 4,000 French troops arrived by land to take ship for the same place. Their stay in the town, encamped on the banks of Dorsey's, or College, Creek, is commemorated by two monuments, one a simple marker in the Naval Academy grounds, the other a beautiful bronze relief on the bluff behind St. John's College, erected to mark the spot where a number who died were buried. As Ambassador Jusserand said in dedicating the monument, this was the first of the memorials to "unknown soldiers" of wars in which the two nations took part.

No place in the Colonies was perhaps better adapted to give the French officers a sympathetic reception. Annapolis was in America what Paris was in France, the center of fashion, refinement and luxury. As the Abbé Robin, a chaplain in the French army, said after visiting it at this time:

"That very inconsiderable town . . . out of the few buildings it contains, has at least three-fourths such as may be styled elegant and grand. Female luxury here exceeds what is known in the provinces of France; a French hairdresser is a man of importance among them, and it is said a certain dame here hires one of that craft at a thousand crowns a year salary. The State House is a very beautiful building, I think the most so of any I have seen in America. The peristyle is set off with pillars, and the edifice is topped with a dome." [1]

It is not strange, therefore, that the French

[1] C. C. Robin, "New Travels Through America," Letter IX.

were delighted with Annapolis, or that the townspeople reciprocated the feeling. On June 25, 1781, the birth of an heir to the French throne had been celebrated with a public dinner of many toasts, a salute of five hundred cannon, and a splendid ball.

In 1782, after the surrender of Cornwallis, French troops were quartered in many places in Maryland, and Annapolis saw much of the young aristocratic Frenchmen who were on the staffs of Rochambeau and his subordinate commanders. Baron de Closen, one of these, a youth of only twenty when he wrote in 1782, records in his journal, now among the Rochambeau Papers in the Library of Congress, how he accompanied Rochambeau to Annapolis in July. At that time Lafayette was in the city with a body of troops waiting transportation to France.

"Before the war," he writes, "Annapolis was very strong commercially, and the richest people of the State made it their home, which brought it about that here society was charming and boasted some very pretty women, very well brought up, quite wealthy, and fond of social life. Madame Lloyd [wife of Richard Bennett

Lloyd], is surely one of the most beautiful women I have seen in America. She was born in London. Her husband is a rich native of Maryland, who, having been in England studying, begged her in marriage of her parents, and obtained her only on condition that he should spend two years in England while she remained in France. He agreed to this, and it is her stay in France which has given her so many graces and so many of the charming French manners that are hers to such perfection. In her home everything is French, and she dresses with a taste and a distinction which have fascinated us. She also speaks French and Italian perfectly. In a word, she is reputed to be *the* American beauty." [1]

Testimony from the other side is furnished by a letter written by a sprightly Annapolis *chatelaine,* Mrs. Benjamin Ogle, daughter of a rich Marylander and partly a Tory, but wife of the son of Governor Ogle of the 1730's and 40's and himself to be Governor from 1789 to 1801.

---

[1] Translated from the *Maryland Historical Magazine,* September, 1910, pp. 233-4. Mrs. Lloyd's beauty is well attested by her portrait painted by Sir Joshua Reynolds and representing her as Shakespeare's Rosalind. Also by a remark at the end of De Closen's letter, where he refers to her husband as "M. her dear husband, who is jealousy personified."

Writing in March, 1781, she says to a friend of her own sex:

"The town is so dull it would be intolerable were it not for the officers. I sometimes see them, but am not acquainted with many. I scarcely ever see or hear the name of a gentleman of our former acquaintance. 'Tis all marquises, counts, etc. One very clever French colonel I have seen. I like the French better every hour. The divine Marquis de la Fayette is in town, and is quite the thing. We abound in French officers, and some of them are very clever, particularly the colonel before mentioned. But the marquis—so diffident, so polite, in short everything that is clever. I have seen one *tolerable* American among them, a Major Macpherson, one of the marquis's family; perhaps that has polished him. The British ships are still here, and a great number of boats, with troops on board, are gone out to-day, and I expect every moment to hear the cannon. Everybody seems quite anxious to know the fate of this day."[1]

A similar impression is made on her cousin, Ann Dulany, in Baltimore and Annapolis dur-

[1] *Atlantic Monthly*, November, 1890, p. 651 ff.

ing these years. She writes in December, 1781, that:

"A few days ago I had the pleasure of three French gentlemen (real gentlemen) to drink tea with me. One of them was a Count Somebody with a hard name; a very elegant man of fashion, one might see it at once. He holds his commission under the French King, and not under King Con."[1]

And in April, 1782, Ann Dulany writes in a similar strain:

"Several Frenchmen visit me, and I find them agreeable. They are all easy and polite, and ready to oblige. They say the Tories are the people of fashion at least and they love and pity them for all their sufferings. This is French flattery, some may think. But I beg leave to differ with all such. Because, when we reflect on their great loyalty and attachment to their king (and love for all kings in general), and their very great contempt for the rulers of this land, I believe them sincere."

It is interesting to note that the latter lady in the year that followed married a Frenchman

[1] *Atlantic Monthly*, November, 1890, p. 651 ff.

and left America never to return. A witness of the scenes of the French Revolution, she and her husband were compelled to flee to England, where she spent her last days. And even in 1784, when Congress was in session in Annapolis, her cousin, Mrs. Benjamin Ogle, is still ·charmed with the French. She writes to her friend in Bladensburg, to whom all the letters are directed, as follows:

"I assure you the town is very agreeable. The minister (probably the French minister) has been here two weeks, and two agreeable men with him, and a gay French officer, General Armand, with whom I danced last night at a ball where there were sixty ladies. Our friend (probably Governor Eden) was there in scarlet and gold, and looked like himself. You know I always thought him superior to most. We supped with him two nights ago, a snug party. Generally dine once a week with the president (probably General Mifflin, President of Congress, and a connection by marriage of the Dulanys). The last time was day before yesterday with forty. I must now lay down my pen for some time, as I am told the prettiest fellow in the world is below, to whom I hope soon to introduce you."[1]

Probably the gayety due to the French officers was highest during 1782-3, for on January 4, 1783, Count Rochambeau spent a night in Annapolis and the next morning embarked on board the *L'Emeraude* on his return to France. But many French remained, for on the 23d of April we hear of "an infinity of French beaux" from a letter written by the widow of Walter Dulany, who was then a woman with married sons and daughters, to her son Walter, who had sought refuge in England from the wrath of the patriots and had not yet returned. She writes from Annapolis in part as follows:

"My dear Wat:

". . . Thursday our races begin and Kitty (her daughter) has just gone off in a superb phaeton-and-four with a very flaming beau to the ground. I don't know his name. Yesterday was his first appearance with our infinity of French beaux, all of whom are very gallant. . . .

"We have a dismal set of players too, who will act every night of this joyous week.

[1] *Atlantic Monthly*, November, 1890, p. 651 ff.

"To-morrow we celebrate Peace (the signing of the treaty of peace between England and the United States). I hear there is to be a grand dinner on Squire Carroll's Point, a whole ox to be roasted, and I can't tell how many sheep and calves, besides a world of other things. Liquor in proportion. The whole to conclude with illuminations and squibbs, etc. I had like to have forgot to mention the ball, which I think had better be postponed. I am horribly afraid our gentlemen will have lighter heads than heels. I think to keep myself snug at home and pray no mischief may happen and for Kitt's safe return from the Ball. . . .

". . . The shoes, etc., came very opportunely for Kitty, just two days before our gaiety commences. They are very pretty. You must accept her thanks thro' me, as she is entirely taken up at present and will be for several days. Be pleased to accept my thanks for the very pretty handkerchief. I'll wear it and think of you.

"I am, my dear Wat, Y'r affect. Mother,

M. DULANY."[1]

[1] E. H. Murray, "One Hundred Years Ago," pp. 67-8 (Letters of the Dulany and Addison Families).

Lafayette and Rochambeau 189

Though Lafayette had returned to France after the Revolution he came back to the United States in 1784, and on November 28th reached Annapolis in the company of Washington himself. The two Houses of the Legislature being then in session, both presented him with addresses of welcome, and Lafayette returned the following answer:

"Gentlemen: On this opportunity so pleasantly anticipated, of my respectful congratulations to your General Assembly, I meet such precious marks of your partiality, as most happily complete my satisfaction.

"Amidst the enjoyments of allied successes, affection conspires with interest to cherish a mutual intercourse; and in France you will ever find that sympathizing good will, which leaves no great room for private exertions. With the ardor of a most zealous heart, I earnestly hope this State, ever mindful of the public spirit she has conspicuously displayed, will to the fullest extent improve her natural advantages, and in the Federal Union so necessary to all, attain the highest degree of particular happiness and prosperity.

"While you are pleased, gentlemen, to consider my life as being devoted to the service of humanity, I feel not less gratified by so flattering an observation than by your friendly wishes for its welfare, and the pleasure I now experience in presenting you with the tribute of my attachment and gratitude.

La Fayette."

Anxious to do him further honor, the Assembly by legislative enactment made Lafayette and his male heirs forever natural-born citizens of the State and entitled, upon their conforming to the Constitution and the laws, to all the privileges of native-born citizens. This was pleasantly recalled when Lafayette visited Annapolis in 1824 accompanied by his son, George Washington Lafayette, and also when a later descendant, the Marquis de Chambrun, a French commander who won fame at Verdun, was in the United States at the close of the World War.

CHAPTER XII

WASHINGTON VISITS ANNAPOLIS

REFERENCE has already been made several times to the visits of the Father of His Country to Annapolis, but there are so many of these, begun so early and continued so long, that it will be worth while to bring them together for the light they throw on the personality of Washington, especially because they illuminate a side of his character which has usually been overshadowed by outstanding and public traits as a general and statesman. The records of his life in Annapolis show that his was a well-rounded personality, all the greater for these minor qualities. In Annapolis he appears once as a great military figure, but at other times as the man of fashion, the friendly visitor, and the conscientious husband and stepfather.

To Washington, Annapolis had many attractions which made it a rival even of Williamsburg, to which he was obliged to repair for his duties as a member of the Virginia House of Burgesses or as the commander of its militia in the defense against Indian attacks. Annapolis was nearer, directly on the route to the North, and the center of many commercial, political and social activities in which he was interested. And it was a larger place than the Virginia capital. From Mount Vernon Washington would cross the Potomac to Port Tobacco on the Maryland side, and then ride on through Upper Marlborough across the South River to Annapolis, a comfortable day's journey. From Annapolis, or in returning to Mount Vernon from Philadelphia, he would use the easy stretch of water with its regular ferry between the Maryland capital and Rock Hall or Chestertown on the eastern shore of the Chesapeake.

Questions of military co-operation between Maryland and Virginia probably first brought Washington to Annapolis, for the letters between him and Governor Sharpe are numerous, and we have a record of his presence in the town on February 14, 1757. There is even an interesting tale, which may be true, that he was entertained at White Hall by Governor Sharpe about this time, and that he danced there with Mary Ridout, sister of John Ridout, while Benjamin Franklin, who was in Annapolis on some errand at the same time, played the tune on the musical glasses.

By the year 1770, however, Washington had become a leading character in the southern colonies, and as a man of wealth and social standing became a fairly frequent visitor, for now Annapolis was distinctly the social center of the section that lay along the shores of the Chesapeake and the Potomac. Several visits are recorded in detail in the diaries that Washington, so methodical in all things, kept. They reveal the manner of the life he led and show his enjoyment of all the various social activities of the period, the club, the races, the theater, the ball, and—the one which seems to have engrossed the time and strength of gentlemen of the period more than any other—the dinner table. We also learn the breadth of his acquaintance in both Tory and patriot circles, for he seemed to know everybody.

Besides the diaries which are to-day lovingly preserved in the Division of Manuscripts of the

Annapolis

Library of Congress, there are also to be found in the same place the ledgers in which Washington kept the accounts of Mount Vernon and his own personal expenses from 1754 on. We are enabled therefore to reproduce not only the records of his movements from his diaries but also the intimate details of his travelling expenses, his gifts to servants, his losses and winnings at cards, and his bets at the races. These records as far as they relate to Annapolis follow:

[Sept.] 21 [1771]. Set out with Mr. Wormeley for the Annapolis races—dined at Mr. William Digges's and lodged at Mr. Ignatius Digges's.

22. Dined at Mr. Samuel Galloway's and lodged with Mr. Boucher in Annapolis.

23. Dined with Mr. Lloyd Dulany and spent the evening at the Coffee House.

24. Dined with the Governor and went to the play and ball afterwards.

25. Dined at Dr. Stewart's and went to the play and ball afterwards.

26. Dined at Mr. Ridout's and went to the play after it.

27. Dined at Mr. Carroll's and went to the ball.

28. Dined at Mr. Boucher's and went from thence to the play and afterwards to the Coffee House.

29. Dined with Major Jenifer and supped at Daniel Dulany, Esqr's.

THE OLD SENATE CHAMBER, STATE HOUSE
The bronze tablet in the floor marks the spot where Washington stood when he resigned his commission in 1783

Washington Visits Annapolis

30. Left Annapolis and dined and supped with Mr. Samuel Galloway.

Oct. 1. Dined at Upper Marlborough and reached home in the afternoon, Mr. Wormeley, Mr. Fitzhugh, Mr. Randolph, Mr. Burwell, and Jack Custis came with me—found Mr. Pendleton here.

1771	Contra [Cash paid out][1]	£.	s.	d.
Sept. 19	By expenses to and from Annapolis races	2	16	7
23	By John Parke Custis at ye Annapolis races	8	—	—
	By a pair of shoes for my servant	—	8	—
	By a velvet cap for ditto	1	4	—
	By cards different times	13	4	8
	By play tickets at ditto	3	—	—
	By ball ditto	—	18	—

[Oct.] 4 [1772]. Set off for the Annapolis races—dined and lodged at Mr. Boucher's.

5. Reached Annapolis—dined at the Coffee House with the Jockey Club and lodged at the Governor's after going to the play.

6. Dined at Major Jenifer's—went to the ball and supped at the Governor's.

7. Dined at the Governor's and went to the play afterwards.

8. Dined at Col. Lloyd's and went to the play—from thence early to my lodgings.

---

[1] **Washington's Ledgers, 1750-1784, Ledger "A", Library of Congress, folio 345.**

9. Dined at Mr. Ridout's—went to the play and to the Governor's to supper.

10. Dined wtih Mr. Carroll of Carrollton—and set out for Mr. Boucher's, which place I arrived at about eight o'clock.

11. Got home to a late dinner—John Parke Custis came with me—found Mrs. Barnes there.

1772 October	Contra[1] [cash paid out]	£.	s.	d.
	By expenses of a trip to and from the Annapolis races—travelling	2	10	11
	By servants on the trip	—	17	—
	By sundry tickets to the plays there	1	—	—
	By ditto ditto to the ball ditto	—	12	—
7	By cash paid Mr. Samuel Galloway for 2 boxes of claret containing 12 dozen	20	14	—
	By ditto paid Col. Ab. Barnes for the horse Dr. Craik bought for me of his son John £.50 Maryland Currency equal to	40	—	—
	By charity	2	3	—
10	By cash lost on the races	1	6	—
	By ditto paid for a hat for Miss Custis	4	4	—
	By ditto paid Mr. Custis at Annapolis	2	14	—

[1] *Ibid.*, Ledger "B," folio 60.

[April] 12 [1773]. Set off for Annapolis with Mr. Custis—dined and lodged at Mr. Boucher's with Governor Eden and others.

13. Got to Annapolis—dined and lodged at the Governor's—where I also supped.

14. Dined and supped at Mr. Lloyd Dulany's—lodged at the Governor's.

15. Dined at Col. Sharpe's and returned to Annapolis—supped and lodged at the Governor's.

16. Dined and supped at Mr. Daniel Dulany's—lodged at the Governor's.

17. Left Annapolis — dined and lodged at Mr. Boucher's.

18. Reached home to dinner after passing through Piscataway Town.

1773	Contra[1] [cash paid out]	£.	s.	d.
April 10	By expenses in Annapolis	1	1	4
	By Mr. Custis's ditto	—	18	—
	By ferriage going and returning there	—	8	6
	By servant there	1	1	—
	By charity	—	1	6
17	By fee to Mr. Thomas Johnson in my attach—against D. Jenifer's Adam	2	5	—
	By cash paid for a horse	8	—	—
	By ditto to Mr. Custis	4	12	—

[1] *Ibid.*, folio 88.

[May] 13 [1773]. Those two gentlemen stayed to dinner, after which I set out on my journey for New York—lodged at Mr. Calvert's.

11. Breakfasted at Mr. Ignatius Digges's—dined at the Coffee House in Annapolis and lodged at the Governor's.

12. Dined, supped, and lodged at the Governor's.

13. After breakfast and about eight o'clock set out for Rock Hall, where we arrived in two hours and twenty-five minutes—dined on board the *Annapolis* at Chestertown and supped and lodged at Mr. Reynolds's.

[Sept.] 26 [1773]. I set off for Annapolis races—dined at Rollins's and got to Annapolis between five and six o'clock—spent the evening and lodged at the Governor's.

27. Dined at the Governor's and went to the play in the evening.

28. Again dined at the Governor's and went to the play and ball in the evening.

29. Dined at Mr. Sprigg's and went to the play in the evening.

30. Dined at Mr. Ridout's and spent the afternoon and evening at Mr. Jenifer's.

Oct. 1. Still at Annapolis—dined with Mr. Ogle—spent the evening at the Governor's.

2. Set off on my return home—dined at Marlborough and lodged at home—Mr. Custis coming with me.

1773 Sept.	Contra[1] [cash paid out]	£.	s.	d.
23	By travel and expenses to and from the Annapolis races	4	16	10
	By sundry play tickets		3	6 —
	By a ticket to the ball		—	6 —
	By cards and racing		3	16 —
	By servants		1	15 3
		14	—	1
	By cash paid for Mr. Custis's expenses there		3	— —
	By a pair of black silk hose		—	18 —

The races often seem to have determined the times of Washington's visits, and he even records the very bets he made and the losses he suffered. But he seems to have never allowed himself the expensive luxury of a racing stable, although he was fond of fox hunting and kept several good horses for that purpose. The races, however, were the occasion for many other social events. It was then that the theater was

[1] *Ibid.,* folio 94.

open, it was then that balls were given, and generally the provincial court was in session, and there was opportunity for business as well as pleasure.

When we remember that Washington was not, like many Marylanders, educated in England, or even the recipient of a college education in Virginia, like Jefferson, but was from early years more familiar with the wilderness and the camp than with the ball room and the senate chamber, it is not too much to infer that his visits to the elegant and cultivated society of Annapolis did much to refine and polish the exterior as well as broaden the intellectual outlook of the somewhat reticent self-made Virginia colonel, and prepare him to achieve success and maintain prestige on the larger stage of the Revolution.

In many ways it is probable that Washington had much in common with the leaders of the Maryland patriots in their rather reluctant conversion to the idea of independence. He had, of course, joined the agreement not to import any article on which a tax had been laid, for we find him in 1769 writing to his London agent directions not to ship any such. In 1774, when the later non-importation agreement was under discussion, he, like one hundred and thirty-five citizens of Annapolis, protested against the provision by which debts due English firms were not to be paid.

One interest which Washington had in Annapolis before the Revolution centered in Rev. Jonathan Boucher, rector of St. Anne's from 1770 to 1772, and one of the most interesting characters of the period. Boucher had come to Virginia in 1759 as a tutor, had later studied divinity and received ordination in England. When he returned to Virginia he not only carried on the duties of a parish priest, but conducted a small boys' school, one of his pupils being John Parke Custis, son of Mrs. Washington by her first marriage. She seems, however, to have left the education of her son almost wholly in her husband's hands.

When Boucher secured a parish in Maryland, where livings paid rather better than in Virginia, he carried Custis along with him, and even brought him along with him to Annapolis when he came to St. Anne's in 1770. But Boucher, as a bachelor, found it difficult to secure suitable living accommodations in Annapolis at first, and the work of attending to his clerical duties, superintending the teaching of several boys and guarding them against the temptations of the provincial capital was apparently too much for Boucher's abilities. As a result Washington complains of the slight progress his ward is making, and Boucher paints Custis as lacking in all ambition. The letters were frequent and show Washington's conscientious attention to the matter as well as a feeling on his part that education is one thing which he does not entirely understand and that Mrs. Washington's fondness for her son makes remedial measures all the more difficult. Yet he shows the greatest solicitude for her feelings, especially when Boucher takes Custis to Baltimore to be inoculated against small-pox. Washington wishes it done without his wife's knowledge as it will make her anxious and prevent her travelling to Williamsburg as she had planned. And he urges that every precaution be taken to prevent any disastrous consequences.

Washington's letter to Boucher under date of

December 16, 1770, shows his earnest wish for Custis's welfare. It reads:

"Mount Vernon, Dec. 16th, 1770.

"According to appointment Jacky Custis now returns to Annapolis. His mind [is] a good deal released from study, and more than ever turned to dogs, horses, and guns; indeed upon dress and equipage, which till of late, he has discovered little inclination of giving in to. I must beg the favor of you, therefore, to keep him close to those useful branches of learning which he ought now to be acquainted with, and as much as possible under your own eye. Without these, I fear he will too soon think himself above control, and be not much the better for the extraordinary expense attending his living in Annapolis; which I should be exceedingly sorry for, as nothing but a hasty progress towards the completion of his education can justify my keeping him there at such an expense as his estate will now become chargeable with.

"The time of life he is now advancing into requires the most friendly aid and counsel (especially in such a place as Annapolis); otherwise, the warmth of his own passions, assisted by the bad example of other youth, may prompt him to actions derogatory of virtue and that innocence of manners which one could wish to preserve him in; for which reason I would beg leave to request that he may not be suffered to sleep from under your own roof unless it be at such places as you are sure he can have no bad examples set him; nor allow him to be rambling about of nights in company with those who do not care how debauched and vicious his conduct may be.

"You will be so good, I hope, as to excuse the liberty I have taken in offering my sentiments thus freely—I have his well-being much at heart and should be sorry to see him fall into any vice or evil course which there is a possibility of restraining him from." [1]

In a letter less than a month later Washington expresses with considerable hesitation his ideas on the most desirable studies. He writes:

"In respect to the kinds and manner of his studying, I leave it wholly to your better judgment—had he begun, or rather pursued his study

[1] Ford, "Writings of Washington," vol. II, p. 316.

of the Greek language, I should have thought it no bad acquisition; but whether [if] he acquire it now he may not forego some more useful branches of learning, is a matter worthy of consideration. To be acquainted with the French tongue is become a part of polite education; and to a man who has [the prospect] of mixing in a large circle absolutely [necessary. Without] arithmetic the common [affairs of] life are not to be managed [with success. The study of geo] metry and the mathe[matics (with due regard to the li]mits of it) is equally [advantageous. The principles] of philosophy, moral, natural, etc. I should think a very desirable knowledge for a gentleman; but as I said before, I leave the whole to your direction; with this earnest request that in whatever kind of study you think proper to engage him he may be kept diligently to it, for he really has no time to lose." [1]

Boucher's picture of the fifteen-year old youth is not promising for his development in Annapolis. "I must confess to you," he writes to Washington, "I never did in my life know a youth so exceedingly indolent, or so surprisingly volup-

[1] *Ibid.*, vol. II, p. 319.

tuous: one would suppose nature had intended him for some Asiatic prince." Later in the letter he writes a long explanation of the difficulties Custis is under. He says:

"It is, possibly, a misfortune to him that everywhere much notice is taken of him. Whether this may be owing to his family, his fortune, his manners, or his connexions, or all together, I will not now enquire. But this is certain, that tho' I am often pleased with it, yet it is the source of infinite disquietude to me. It is here as with you: he has many invitations to visits, balls, and other scenes of pleasure, to which neither you nor I can refuse his going—more especially if we go ourselves. Indeed, I do not know that it would be right to refuse, even if good manners would allow it. Yet so it is, he seldom or never goes abroad without learning something I could have wished him not to have learned. There are not, that I know of, more idle or pleasurable people in Annapolis than there are in any other town containing an equal number of inhabitants: yet somehow or other he has contrived to learn a great deal of idleness and dissipation among them. One inspires him with a passion for dress—another for racing, fox hunting, etc.—even the grave Col. Sharpe, you see, led him to talk of guns and rifles with much more satisfaction than I can persuade him to talk of books or literary subjects."[1]

When some discussion arose as to the value of a European tour for Custis, Boucher wrote much advice and proposed himself as his companion. Boucher argues that while it may be expensive— and he states that Mr. Dulany says his son spent £500 in Paris in three months—yet if he remained at home and fell into some such habit as dealing in horses, or "but in a very moderate degree, sporting, as it is called, neither of which he could well avoid from the general prevalence of example," it would cost him as much. When Governor Eden suggested that there should first be a six months' tour of the colonies, Boucher agreed and hoped that Washington would find time to spend a few months with the party.

The European trip was finally abandoned, and Boucher moved to a country parish where the emoluments promised better than at St.

[1] Hamilton, "Letters to Washington," vol. IV, p. 42.

Anne's, which seems at this time to have been in very poor condition, a dilapidated church and a living of only about £250 for the rector. Custis was later sent to New York to King's College, now Columbia, but remained only three months. He then returned to Mount Vernon and at the age of nineteen married Eleanor Calvert, aged sixteen, to whom he had become engaged without the consent of either family while he was under Boucher in Annapolis. Although Washington endeavored to postpone the marriage for two or three years till Custis had completed his education and shown his affection to be lasting, they were married in about a year and seem to have lived most happily till Custis's death while serving as an aide-de-camp of Washington in the Yorktown campaign. Through it all Washington's mastery of detail and high sense of duty appear in striking fashion.

Boucher has probably left us the best collection of comments on the principal characters who shone in the society of this section in the years preceding the breaking out of hostilities with the mother country. An enthusiastic pamphleteer and propagandist, he engaged in almost every political and religious controversy of the time, and believed himself to be the most influential and cleverest of those who used the columns of the *Maryland Gazette* or the *Virginia Gazette* to further their causes. Not all of these articles can be identified but in the "Reminiscences" which he left behind him, in the letters which he wrote to Washington, and his correspondence with English friends we have an intensely personal account of the events of his day. Besides, after he returned to England in the early days of the Revolution he prepared and finally published his "A View of the Causes and Consequences of the American Revolution," which had a very considerable influence in forming public opinion in regard to Washington. His letters and other papers were handed to Thackeray and used by him in writing "The Virginians," where one easily recognizes the "shy, silent, stern, slow" Washington such as Boucher pictured, touched though it is with a human sympathy that was Thackeray's own contribution.

At first Boucher's impressions of Annapolis were favorable. "It was," he declares, "the genteelest town in North America, and many of its inhabitants were highly respectable as to station, fortune, and education. I hardly know a town in England so desirable to live in as Annapolis was then." But he soon found St. Anne's a poor living and only desirable as *Gradum ad Parnassum*, a path to preferment, as he calls it on account of its being close to the Governor. Of Governor Sharpe, to whom he had unsuccessfully applied for a parish, he says: "A well-meaning but weak man, and much under the influence of Mr. Ridout, his Secretary." Another time he remarks of him: "He is a hearty, rattling, wild young dog of an officer; he is too, a bit of a scholar—has Horace all by heart, of whom indeed he is a faithful disciple." Of Governor Eden he writes: "A handsome, lively, and sensible man, . . . had been in the Army and had contracted such habits of expense and dissipation as were fatal to his fortune, and at length to his life. Yet with all his follies and foibles, which were indeed abundant, he had such a warmth and affectionativeness of heart that it was impossible not to love him."

Boucher was just that sort of Tory who would

be the victim of popular attack, and it is not strange that in the last six months of his preaching in Maryland he always had a brace of loaded pistols lying on the pulpit ready at hand. Uncompromising in his opposition to the Revolutionary movement, he was haled before the patriot committee in Annapolis, but according to his own account came off with flying colors by virtue of his eloquence. He was one of the few prominent Tories who were formally charged with treason and whose estates were actually confiscated.

A veritable Dean Swift in invective, Boucher wrote to Washington after his flight from the country a letter which is a masterpiece, though it is probable that its sentiments are actuated by political partisanship rather than personal animus. This also accounts for his milder, though uncomplimentary, characterization of Washington in his letters, from which a phrase has already been quoted. Yet the chief passage is worth quoting in full. It reads:

"I did know Mr. Washington well; and though occasion may call forth traits of character that never could have been discovered in the more sequestered scenes of life, I cannot conceive how he could, otherwise than through the interested representations of party, have ever been spoken of as a great man. He is shy, silent, stern, slow, and cautious; but has no quickness of parts, extraordinary penetration, nor an elevated style of thinking. In his moral character he is regular, temperate, strictly just and honest (excepting that as a Virginian he has lately found out that there is no moral turpitude in not paying what he confesses he owes to a British creditor), and, as I always have thought, religious; having heretofore been pretty constant, and even exemplary, in his attendance on public worship in the Church of England. But he seems to have nothing generous or affectionate in his nature. Just before the close of the last war he married the widow Custis, and thus came into the possession of her large jointure. He never had any children, and lived very much like a gentleman at Mount Vernon, in Fairfax County, where the most distinguished part of his character was that he was an admirable farmer."[1]

[1] "Notes and Queries," Series V, vol. V, p. 503.

Washington Visits Annapolis

The opinion of Eddis, who saw Washington at Governor Eden's, is more favorable. "Reserved in conversation," he writes, "but liberal in opinion, his actions have hitherto been directed to calmness and moderation; a perseverance in which conduct may restrain misguided ardor and direct every movement to that grand point,—a permanent and constitutional reconciliation."

There is no record of Washington being in Annapolis, or even passing through it, during the period of the Revolution until November 21, 1781, when on his way to the North after the defeat of Cornwallis he spent one night with Governor Lee in the same structure where he had lodged before with Sir Robert Eden. Then, as says the *Maryland Gazette,* "on his appearance in the streets, people of every rank and every age eagerly pressed forward to feed their eyes with gazing on the man, to whom, under Providence, and the generous aid of our great and good ally, they owed their present security and their hopes of future liberty and peace. The courteous affability with which he returned their salutes lighted up ineffable joy in every countenance and diffused the most animated gratitude through every breast." As usually, a public dinner, an illumination of the city, and a ball in the Assembly Rooms were the necessary honors of the occasion.

The pre-eminent occasion which associates Washington with Annapolis is, however, the resignation of his position as commander-in-chief of the Revolutionary armies. This took place in the Old Senate Chamber of the State House on December 23, 1783. During that year the Congress began meeting alternately in Annapolis and Trenton, and on the 4th of November assembled in the Annapolis State House. As soon as news of the signing of the treaty of peace was received in America General Clinton evacuated New York and Washington occupied the city with his troops. Then, his work done, he hastened to return his commission to Congress and secure relief from his military responsibilities.

When Washington arrived in Annapolis on December 20th, and took up his quarters at Mann's Tavern, he was at once the object of addresses of welcome and appreciation from the

Washington Visits Annapolis 215

Legislature, the City Council, the Governor and his Council, and the citizens of Baltimore. Before he left on the 24th he had been given the usual honors, a public dinner, an illumination, and a ball. As the bill Mr. Mann sent the State for the refreshments served at the ball indicates,—it has somehow survived in the State archives,—the hospitality was unstinted. In all it cost the State £71 6s. 6d. For this was furnished 98 bottles of wine, 2½ gallons of spirits, 9 pounds of sugar, 12 packs of cards, 8 pounds of candles, music, etc.

The actual ceremony of resignation was made very formal, for Congress decided upon the order of precedence in the procession, the order of speeches, and even prescribed that "when the General rises to make his address and also when he retires, he is to bow to Congress, which they are to return by uncovering without bowing."

The historic ceremony, so appealingly portrayed by the artist Trumbull in the well-known painting, took place in the south-east room in the State House, a room now happily restored to almost its original condition and decoration at this time. At the further end of the room on a semi-circular dais stood the chair of the President of Congress, slightly withdrawn into the oval recess of the wall. In a humbler position sat the Clerk before a broad, low desk, the traditional chair and the desk both standing in the identical places to-day. On one side wall stands a huge fireplace, and on the other broad and lofty windows set in a recess with beautifully carved shutters admit a plentiful stream of light. Overhead a huge chandelier for innumerable candles, now reproduced with more modern appliances, was provided for evening sessions.

The members of Congress, about twenty in number, sat in armchairs about the room, with a large table in the space in front of the dais for their convenience when writing. In the gallery over the entrance door sat the wives of the members and other ladies who had been invited to attend, all clustered around the figure of Mrs. Washington, who had come over from Mount Vernon to welcome her husband home and to attend the ceremony. On the floor, crowded around the members of Congress, who were seated with their hats on as indications of the proud sovereignty of the States they represented, were the Governor and his Council, the members of the Legislature, the consul-general of France, the judges of the State courts, and gentlemen from the town and vicinity. At a spot slightly to the right of the presiding officer, and on the floor of the chamber, sat Washington, attended on either side by officers of his staff standing.

The place and the presence were such as stir the imagination and quicken the pulse. The room and building were simple but beautiful, and above the roof was already rising a graceful dome that was to make it the most beautiful colonial building in the country. The town had been the very center of culture and wealth and had shown its patriotic spirit by its vigorous resistance to the earlier measures of oppression and later had carried on a firm but courteous expulsion of British authority. The city and State had done its share with the utmost loyalty to carry on the struggle for liberty, even during the darkest hours of Valley Forge and Trenton. Its first regiments had, on their very arrival, plunged into the Battle of Long Island and left more than half of their numbers in the swamps and on the hillsides of Brooklyn. Its Maryland Line had borne the brunt of British attack in all the battles of the Southern campaign, at Camden, Cowpens, Guilford, and Eutaw Springs, and it had drained its resources to furnish flour and beef to the French and American armies as they enveloped and strangled Cornwallis.

The Assembly itself bore on its rolls the names of men whose deeds are a part of American patriotic tradition. Abiel Foster sat for New Hampshire; Elbridge Gerry, Samuel Osgood, and George Partridge for Massachusetts; William Ellery and David Howell for Rhode Island; Thomas Mifflin and Cadwalader Morris for Pennsylvania; James Tilton and Eleazer McComb for Delaware; James McHenry and Edward Lloyd for Maryland; Thomas Jefferson, Samuel Hardy, Arthur Lee, and James Monroe for Virginia; Benjamin Hawkins, Hugh Williamson, and Richard Dobbs Spaight for North Carolina, and South Carolina was represented by Jacob Read.

Though Alexander Hamilton had been elect-

WASHINGTON, LAFAYETTE, AND TENCH TILGHMAN
Painted by Charles Willson Peale in 1785. Now in Old Senate Chamber

ed from New York, as well as John Hall, Thomas Stone, and Samuel Chase from Maryland, none of them had presented themselves and become qualified to take part in the deliberations. The last two named, though not members of Congress, are generally credited with having been present, as well as the other two Maryland signers of the Declaration of Independence, Charles Carroll and William Paca. The last was Governor and had a prominent place in the reception given Washington, even the chairs from his home being taken to the State House for use on the occasion.

In addition to Washington himself, there were present his military aides, probably David Humphries, William S. Smith, Henry Baylis, and certainly Tench Tilghman, who in a ride that has gone down in history carried the news of Yorktown through Annapolis to the Congress in Philadelphia. Furthermore, three days earlier Generals Horatio Gates and William Smallwood had welcomed their commander-in-chief to the Maryland capital and were presumably present at his resignation.

But the central figure was Washington himself. With a fortune almost providential, he had commanded the armies of the colonists from the very beginning through more than eight years of struggle. He had won few spectacular victories, few dramatic successes. But with slender forces and pitifully inadequate supplies he had held the British to the chief seaports, directed the operations of armies as far separated as those of Gates at Saratoga and Greene in South Carolina, had never allowed himself to be decisively defeated, and had persisted till France saw fit to link her fortunes with the revolted colonies and with the troops of Rochambeau and the fleet of De Grasse help to achieve a victory sufficiently discouraging to British pride to produce a cessation of hostilities and a recognition of independence.

At noon of the 23rd of December, in such a presence as has been described, General Mifflin, the President of Congress, rose and informed Washington that "the United States in Congress assembled are prepared to receive your communication." With equal formality but with such feeling that he could with difficulty enunciate, Washington rose, and, standing on the spot marked to-day by a bronze plate, read the following address:

"Mr. President:

"The great events on which my resignation depended having at length taken place, I have now the honor of offering my sincere congratulations to Congress, and of presenting myself before them, to surrender into their hands the trust committed to me and to claim the indulgence of retiring from the service of my country.

"Happy in the confirmation of our independence and sovereignty, and pleased with the opportunity afforded the United States of becoming a respectable nation, I resign with satisfaction the appointment I accepted with diffidence; a diffidence in my abilities to accomplish so arduous a task, which, however, was superseded by a confidence in the rectitude of our cause, the support of the supreme power of the Union and the patronage of Heaven.

"The successful termination of the war has verified the most sanguine expectations; and my gratitude for the interposition of Providence and the assistance I have received from my countrymen increases with every review of the momentous contest.

"While I repeat my obligations to the army in general, I should do injustice to my own feelings not to acknowledge in this place the peculiar services and distinguished merits of the gentlemen who have been attached to my person during the war. It was impossible the choice of confidential officers to compose my family should have been more fortunate. Permit me, Sir, to recommend in particular those who have continued in the service to the present moment as worthy of the favorable notice and patronage of Congress.

"I consider it an indispensable duty to close this last act of my official life by commending the interests of our dearest country to the protection of Almighty God and those who have the superintendence of them to His holy keeping.

"Having now finished the work assigned me, I retire from the great theater of action, and bidding an affectionate farewell to this august body under whose orders I have so long acted,

I here offer my commission, and take my leave of all the employments of public life."

As Washington concluded his speech, he handed his commission and a copy of the address to the President, who responded in well chosen words of gratitude and affection, beginning: "The United States in Congress assembled receive, with emotions too affecting for utterance, the solemn resignation of the authorities under which you have led their troops with success through a perilous and doubtful war,"— words penned, it is said, by Jefferson for the occasion.

The next morning Washington, now a private citizen, left for Mount Vernon, where he arrived on Christmas Eve. As he wrote to George Clinton, he doubtless revealed his real feelings when he said, "The scene is at last closed. I feel myself eased of a load of public care. I hope to spend the remainder of my days in cultivating the affections of good men and in the practice of the domestic virtues."

A simple but touching picture of the scene and of the feelings which it inspired is found in a letter written by an Annapolitan lady, Mrs. John Ridout, to her mother, Mrs. Samuel Ogle, about a month after the event. She says: "I went with others to see General Washington resign his commission. The Congress was assembled in the State House, both Houses of Assembly were present as spectators, the gallery full of ladies.

"The General seemed so much affected himself that everybody felt for him. He addressed Congress in a short speech, but very affecting. Many tears were shed. He has retired from all public business and designs to spend the rest of his days at his own seat. I think the world never produced a greater man and very few so good." [1]

[1] Lady Edgar, "A Colonial Governor in Maryland," p. 276. The name of Jeremiah Townley Chase should be added to the list of members of Congress from Maryland, and he was presumably present at Washington's resignation.

CHAPTER XIII

IN GENTEEL ECLIPSE

WITH the departure of the French armies and the rapid economic development of the post-Revolutionary period, Annapolis suffered a decline which was noticeable to every traveller who visited the city. The settlement of the western parts of Maryland and the extension of the settled area even to the Ohio and beyond gave Baltimore, which was geographically the *entrepôt* and outlet for these sections, an advantage it soon exhibited by surpassing the capital city. It soon began to draw away the chief citizens, such as Samuel Chase, Charles Carroll of Carrollton, and Charles Carroll the Barrister. Tobacco no longer occupied the place in Maryland's economic life that it once did, the lands in the vicinity of the Severn had been worn out by the exhausting cultivation that resulted, and wheat raising, for which the newer areas closer to the Blue Ridge were suitable, now assumed a more important place. All this destroyed the commercial supremacy of the town on the Severn.

Socially the backbone of Annapolis had been the Tories. Now that their power was over, their lands and wealth confiscated, and their members, many of them, settled in foreign parts, never to return, there was little hope that the brilliancy and luxury of that régime would be restored. Besides, there was already arising among the patriots and their descendants a spirit of democracy which was to play havoc with aristocratic traditions and introduce into American life a brusqueness and plainness which would destroy all class distinctions and make the typical American the very antithesis of the cultivated and foppish imitation of the eighteenth century Englishman which was seen in Annapolis before the break with the mother country.

Politically, however, Annapolis retained its prestige better than in any other way. In spite of occasional attempts on the part of Baltimore to have the seat of government moved there, it remained the capital of the State and the residence of the Governor. For a while indeed it became, as we have seen, the seat of the Congress under the Articles of Confederation, for on the 26th of November, 1783, Congress assembled here and continued in session until June 3, 1784. This had been secured by the efforts of James McHenry, who wrote to Governor Paca to know if the public buildings would be placed at its disposal. "Suit the price of boarding," he urges, "to the economical taste of the Eastern gentlemen."

It was while Congress was sitting here that it received official notification of the signing of a definitive treaty of peace with Great Britain, and it was here, on January 14, 1784, that it formally ratified the treaty. We have already dwelt upon the most important ceremony of the session, Washington's resigning his commission.

While the subject of a permanent capital for the country was under discussion, Annapolis made some efforts to secure the honor. The State buildings were to be offered to the United States and thirteen houses were to be erected for the accommodation of the representatives of the thirteen States. Furthermore, the city authorities declared themselves willing to be placed under the jurisdiction of the central government and be separated from the State. But nothing came of it. When the new capital was laid out on the banks of the Potomac it is interesting to note that the plan of Annapolis, a central circle from which the other streets led out in a "singular and whimsical manner," like rays from a center, was reproduced.

Perhaps the other important event that occurred during this period was the meeting of commissioners from several States in 1786 to discuss commercial restrictions, — a meeting which led directly to the Constitutional Convention of 1787. As it turned out that Virginia added an invitation to all the States to attend and seemed to wish to bring up other matters which would increase the power of Congress, Maryland failed to appoint commissioners. Thus on September 11, 1786, when the commissioners assembled it was found that only five States were represented, though four others had made appointments. Among the twelve men present, however, were such able leaders as Alexander Hamilton, John Dickinson, Edmund Randolph, and James Madison. Partly on account of the small attendance, and partly because its members saw that any thorough reform in the regulation of commerce must require a radical change in the Articles of Confederation, the convention recommended that the States call a constitutional convention in Philadelphia the following May and proceed to redraft their scheme of government. When that body met, the only Annapolitan nominated as a delegate had declined to serve and Annapolis was not represented,—an indication of its declining prestige.

The chief importance of Annapolis after these events seems to have been to act as the most convenient entrance to the new capital city on the Potomac as soon as that was established. Foreign ministers and our own, both of whom commonly travelled on ships of war, arrived or departed by way of Annapolis, and the traditions of hospitality which Annapolis seems to have been noted for were thus given exercise. As the Duc de la Rochefoucault-Liancourt wrote in 1796, when he visited the town,

"The capitalists, or those who have become rich, have quitted it to go and reside at Baltimore, and the inhabitants are in general families in easy circumstances who have property in the neighborhood, officers of the government, and gentlemen of the law, attracted by the vicinity of the courts of justice. The population diminishes every year; the houses are for the most part built of brick, and are spacious; many of them are very large and have fine gardens, in better order than any I have yet seen in America.

"Annapolis is . . . as to society, one of the most agreeable cities of the United States; hospitality and an obliging sincerity are in no part so general; all the families are united, and a stranger, always well received among them, soon finds himself at his ease there."[1]

Since the Revolution two improvements had been made in the appearance of the city. The dome which still surmounts the State House was erected and in place by the time Washington resigned his commission, but the interior work on it was not completed till about 1793. The dome has been criticized by some architects as being unduly high for its diameter, but all

[1] "Travels in North America," vol. III, p. 579.

seem to agree that the lines and decoration of its interior as one gazes up into it from the first floor of the building are extremely beautiful. Indeed, situation and approach probably have as much to do with one's delight in viewing the State House as the details of the building. Placed upon the highest hill and seen at the end of all the streets which radiate from it, the slender dome and the simple lines of the building, its tall-pillared entrance breaking the monotony of its front, it is an object that fascinates the eye of every visitor and delights his sense of beauty. And whether approaching the town by land or water it is the first object of notice.

After the Revolution, also, a new church for St. Anne's Parish was erected, and by 1792 occupied by the congregation which had for nearly twenty years worshipped in the Hallam Theater. As travellers remarked, its size was adapted to its position as a State church and a growing parish, so that after the town began its decline it was far too large for the number of worshipers. And it had lost all the revenue it formerly secured from taxes. During the transition period between the overthrow of the Establishment and the organization of an American Episcopal Church, all churches were neglected and the rectors not always desirable. Many of them seem to have been pleasant companions and educated men, but with little earnestness in religion. Mr. Higginbotham, rector of St. Anne's at this time, was said to have been very fond of card playing. One Sunday morning while he was preaching he started to pull his handkerchief from his pocket, when streaming down from the high pulpit to the floor came a pack of cards which had been deposited there. And for a clergyman after performing the marriage ceremony at the house of the bride, where weddings were almost invariably celebrated, to play the fiddle for the dance was not uncommon.

From this period—1785, to be exact—dates the organization of Methodism in the town, although as early as 1746 Whitefield preached here in the open air, probably under the Liberty Poplar. Francis Asbury, the real founder of American Methodism, also visited the city frequently after 1773. The most prominent pastor

In Genteel Eclipse 233

of the early days, when the society worshiped in the State Armory, was Jesse Lee, the first Methodist preacher in Boston.

The most distinguished product of Annapolis in the days between the end of the War of Independence and the Civil War was William Pinkney, born in Annapolis in 1764 of a Tory family whose entire property was confiscated. He grew up in Baltimore, where he became a protégé of Samuel Chase and studied law in the latter's office. Soon a leader at the Bar of Maryland he was sent in 1805 with James Monroe to England to secure settlements of claims for American vessels seized by the British during the wars with Napoleon. He remained in London prosecuting this mission till 1811, and his letters to Madison are especially valuable pictures of the difficulties in which neutrals were involved and which led finally to the War of 1812. He returned in the frigate *Essex* to Annapolis and began again the practice of law, but was soon appointed Attorney-General of the United States. Unlike most of his friends in Annapolis, he was a strong supporter of the party of Jefferson and Madison, the Republicans, and even fought at Bladensburg in the attempt to defend Washington in 1814.

In 1816, while in Congress, he was made Minister to St. Petersburg, but returned to Baltimore in 1818 and practiced law till his death in 1822. One of his most celebrated arguments was for the United States Bank in 1819 when Maryland attempted to tax it. Though a member of the Jeffersonians politically, his Tory ancestry and his long residence in European capitals inclined him to a fashionableness of dress which made him unpopular in some American circles. He is perhaps a true son of the old era in Annapolis, aristocratic in dress and manner, sensitive to all the niceties of polite society, keenly intellectual, as a lawyer eloquent and convincing, and noted for his use of language of the greatest felicity. The only dwelling in Annapolis which can be named as associated with him is the colonial structure on Charles Street opposite the home of Jonas Green, where tradition says he once lived. His brother, Ninian, as has been mentioned earlier, was one of the line of the owners of the Harwood House.

In Genteel Eclipse 235

The decade following the Revolution also saw in Annapolis the beginning of a change in the mission of the town which has not yet been mentioned, from commerce to education. In colonial times its educational opportunities were centered in King William's School, where Pinkney himself is said to have been a student. With the coming of peace and independence, however, the people of Maryland desired better facilities for intellectual training and projected a State university which should embrace two colleges, one on the Eastern Shore and one on the Western, but both public institutions. In 1782 the Legislature had chartered Washington College at Chestertown and in 1784 granted a charter to a distinguished group of men to establish its western partner. Why the Legislature named it St. John's College has never been satisfactorily explained.

The promoters included such men as Samuel Chase, William Paca, and Charles Carroll of Carrollton, Thomas J. Claggett, recently made Bishop of Maryland, and to emphasize its nonsectarian character Bishop Carroll of the Catholic Church was made President of the Board of Visitors and Governors, while a Presbyterian divine was one of the members. In 1785 the corporation of King William's School united its work and property with the new college, and on November 11, 1789, the institution opened its doors under the principalship of Dr. John McDowell in the building which the Legislature had given it, the ruined Governor's Palace of Thomas Bladen, which had meanwhile been finished and made habitable.

The original charter had granted to the college an appropriation of £1750 annually, but in 1805 the Legislature rescinded its action and almost killed the institution by cutting off all financial aid. This seems to have been due to a fear that the atmosphere of Annapolis was anti-democratic and that the poor man could not send his son there because of the fees required and the rich thus reaped all the advantages. This action produced almost another Dartmouth College case, as the college contended that the Legislature was without power to repeal the charter, the same having been granted in return for various sums of money furnished by friends of the college. But the college authorities were so much in need of funds that they later agreed to waive such legal claims in lieu of another annual appropriation. Another Legislature allowed the question to be taken to court, and the college won its point as to the validity of its contention, but when it tried to collect the money, found its previous action in waiving the point prevented payment of a single dollar.

In 1866, after the college had been in the possession of the Union army as a hospital during the Civil War, Dr. Henry Barnard, the pioneer in American public school education, was made President and reorganized the institution in the six months he was in office. He then resigned to become the United States Commissioner of Education. Apparently his interest in St. John's was due to his hope of making it the apex to a complete State system of education. When, however, he discovered that Maryland was not ripe for such an enterprise, he sought other fields of labor. Among its faculty brought from the North just after the Civil War, when anti-Southern influence controlled the college, was Hiram Corson, who served as a professor of English literature from 1867 to 1870, when he went to Cornell University.

In 1796 Francis Scott Key, author of "The Star Spangled Banner," graduated from St. John's. Though not born in Annapolis, Key spent much of his youth here in the Scott House, where his great aunt, Mrs. Upton Scott, lived. It is said that guests at the house on many occasions saw the young lad, clad in a white nightgown, stand on the landing of the stairs and repeat his evening prayer, a custom which his aunt seems to have insisted upon whatever the occasion. And it was to Annapolis that he returned in 1802, to wed, in the drawing room of the Chase House, Mary Tayloe Lloyd, daughter of its owner at that time.

St. John's also furnishes the last contact of Washington with Annapolis. In 1798 a letter to Dr. McDowell informed him that Washington was sending George Washington Parke Custis to Annapolis to study at the college, he having already spent about a year at Princeton. The boy was seventeen years old and the son of the John Parke Custis who had been the pupil of Jonathan Boucher in the town in 1770.

Washington writes that "Mr. Custis possesses competent talents to fit him for any studies, but they are counteracted by an indolence of mind which renders it difficult to draw them into action. . . . From drinking and gaming he is perfectly free, and if he has a propensity to any other impropriety it is hidden from me. He is generous and regardful of the truth."[1]

On March 12, 1798, Custis wrote his step-grandfather that he had arrived. "Annapolis," he says, "is a very pleasant place. I visited the principal inhabitants while the doctor was here and found them all very kind. Mr. McDowell is a very good and agreeable man. . . . I was so fortunate as to get in with a Mrs. Bruce, a remarkably clever[2] woman, with whom I live very well and contented. There are several clever young men boarding in this house with whom I associate on the most friendly terms." On April 2d Custis writes: "I have received every kindness from the citizens of Annapolis, and could anything heighten my opinion of your

[1] G. W. P. Custis, "Recollections and Private Memoirs of Washington," p. 98.
[2] Probably *clever* used in the sense still prevailing in the South to mean *agreeable*.

character it would be their expressions of esteem and regard."

By June, however, Washington had to write Custis that they had not heard from him directly for five weeks, but that intimations had reached them that he was paying much attention to a certain young lady. It is, he says, "not a time for a *boy of your age* to enter into engagements which might end in sorrow and repentance." Custis's reply four days later is a confession of the truth of the rumors. He declares he is not engaged, but admits he gave the young lady reasons to believe he was attached to her, and he did solicit her affections and hoped to marry her sometime in the future. But he now says she has refused him and that the affair is all over.

The following September Washington has to write Dr. McDowell to keep him, if possible, from falling in love again. "Prevent," he urges, "as much as it can be done, without too great a restraint, a devotion of his time to visitations of the families in Annapolis, which, when carried to excess or beyond a certain point, cannot but tend to divert his mind from

From an etching by E. P. Metour, by permission of E. H. Curlander, Art Dealer, Baltimore

DOCK STREET AND MARKET

study and lead his thoughts to very different objects." At the end of the month Washington writes that Custis does not seem inclined to return to the college and he has decided to keep him at Mount Vernon. The spectacle of the "Father of His Country," after his years of participation in the monumental labor of military command and in the delicate but momentous tasks of statesmanship, expending his failing powers on the details of a school boy's life makes one realize anew the unsparing devotion to duty which Washington best symbolizes.

A cross-section, as it were, of all the various phases of Annapolis in this period before the War of 1812 is afforded us in a journal kept by David B. Warden, Secretary to the American legation in Paris, who spent several days in Annapolis in the summer of 1811 while waiting there to embark on the frigate *Constitution* for passage abroad. He writes:

"I am pleased with this city; it is beautifully situated. . . . The town has a romantic appearance. The houses are thinly scattered over a considerable extent of surface, and intervening gardens and lawns give it a very rural aspect. . . .

"I had often heard of the hospitality of the Annapolitans to strangers, of which I have had many proofs. Mr. Duval was pleased to give me a letter of introduction to Miss Chase, by which means I became acquainted with this amiable family. Mr., Mrs., and Miss Chase left town for some mineral waters, and after their departure I had the pleasure of passing many hours with the two sisters who remained. They are really fine young ladies; interesting in their appearance; gay without coquetry; social, amiable, and enlightened.

. . . .

"The doctor (Dr. Upton Scott) had some employment under the old government, to which, an exception to almost all his countrymen, he remained attached and fled to Ireland during the war, at the end of which he returned to Annapolis to the enjoyment of his property, which the generosity of the inhabitants would not permit them to confiscate, a strong proof of their esteem for the proprietor. This house is neat and elegantly situated and commands a view of that portion of the bay along which vessels ply to and from Baltimore. In Belfast Dr. S. had mixed with the convivial parties of that town, where indulgence in claret, according to his opinion, sowed the seeds of the gout, the only disease with which in his old age he is occasionally afflicted.

"He is fond of botany and has a number of rare plants and shrubs in his greenhouse and garden. I dined there in company with the Governor of the State [Edward Lloyd] and Dr. Murray, a venerable gentleman highly esteemed, the father of Mrs. Mason. In the parlor is a painting of Mrs. Mason and of her sister, Mrs. Lloyd, when very young, with the bust of Dr. Scott before them.

. . . .

"Annapolis appears to me to be a most economical and pleasing place of residence for those who have no particular profession or commercial pursuit; a family can live here much cheaper than in Washington. Vegetables, fish, crabs, and lobsters are purchased at a low rate. A large, elegant house with a garden, belonging to Mr. Pinkney, is offered for four thousand three hundred dollars. A very commodious building of three stories was sold the other day for six hundred dollars. . . . The people are gay and social, free from the anxiety and cares of commercial operations."[1]

A concluding word should be spoken for two natives of Annapolis who won more than local fame in the period between the Revolution and the Civil War. Dr. John Shaw, whose birthplace was the quaint Dutch colonial house which still stands opposite the State House, achieved some fame as a poet. Reverdy Johnson, Attorney-General of the United States under Zachary Taylor, and the American minister who had a prominent part in the negotiations with England over the *Alabama* claims, was born in the Bordley House, already described, and lived in later life in the old hip-roofed dwelling which still remains opposite the Post Office on Northwest Street.

[1] *Maryland Historical Magazine*, vol. XI, p. 129 ff.

CHAPTER XIV

FORT SEVERN BECOMES THE NAVAL ACADEMY

THAT the annals of Annapolis in the nineteenth century pictured for the first fifty years an eclipse and not a decline is due to the fact that just before the middle of the century the United States Naval Academy was established there. Thus to-day the word Annapolis conjures up in the mind as much the institution where the officers of the Navy are trained as it does the colonial city which still remains the capital of Maryland. The story of this sudden change in the fortunes of the little town gives an interesting insight into the caprices of fortune.

If it had not been for the fact that there already existed, and had since 1808, a fort and government reservation surrounded by a high wall at one end of the town it is unlikely that Annapolis would ever have become the *alma mater* of the naval service. And the high wall is an essential part of the picture. It is constantly mentioned in the official documents, and more than the guns of the fort, which were quite useless, was to serve a useful and necessary purpose in restraining the spirits of the young officer-to-be.

The fort was erected during the year following the outrage upon the United States frigate *Chesapeake,* when just outside the Virginia capes she was stopped by the frigate *Leopard,* and when she resisted a search for seamen who had deserted from British men-of-war, especially the *Melampus,* she was fired upon till she submitted. It happened that the *Melampus* has been cruising in the Chesapeake off Annapolis, blockading some French frigates in the harbor of the town when the desertions occurred. In fact, two of the four men taken from the *Chesapeake* were Marylanders by birth.

During the war of 1812, although the British fleet under Rear Admiral Cockburn sailed up the Chesapeake in 1814 and bombarded Fort McHenry, outside Baltimore, Fort Severn, inadequately manned as it was, seems to have protected the town from attack.

The fort was situated on what was known as Windmill Point, at the junction of the Severn and the harbor of the town, and included eight acres of ground now roughly corresponding to the portion of the Naval Academy grounds lying between the Chapel and the bay side of Bancroft Hall. On it was the former family residence of Walter Dulany, from whose son's heirs the ground was purchased. Fort Severn itself was a cylindrical fort enclosed by a stone wall fourteen feet high, its parapet covered with turf. In an enclosure about a hundred feet in diameter within was a platform about three feet lower than the parapet, and on this eight guns were mounted *en barbette,* that is, with their muzzles exposed above the top of the wall. In the center of the fort was a brick magazine, and shorewards outside the enclosure, a furnace for heating red-hot shot.

To George Bancroft, Secretary of the Navy under President Polk from 1845 to 1846, more than to any other individual, the establishment of a school for the Navy which would do for it what West Point had been doing for nearly fifty years was due. A graduate of Harvard and of Göttingen, already a distinguished historian, Bancroft believed his administration could be no better remembered than by a reform in the method of educating midshipmen for their varied duties.

Up to this time young men securing a midshipman's warrant in the navy had been sent to sea to learn their profession by actual experience. On the larger ships there were "schoolmasters," who were supposed to give instruction in mathematics and navigation, but they had no authority and their students were at the beck and call of any officer. About 1840 two schools had been established, one at Philadelphia and one at Norfolk, where midshipmen preparing for examinations for promotion might secure assistance, but the equipment was scanty and the work interrupted by frequent drafts for sea duty.

After 1841 the school located at the Naval Asylum at Philadelphia forged to the front in efficiency and came to be the only one in real operation. Here were employed three of the instructors with which the Naval Academy was to begin its career. The Naval Asylum, however, being near a large city and in close connection with a navy yard, was not considered a favorable place for a school, and when Secretary Bancroft in 1845 suggested uniting all instruction in one school, he mentioned Fort Severn as a better place. His idea was to make instruction permanent and to send to the school not only all midshipmen preparing for promotion, but all midshipmen on shore duty and all young men who wished to qualify for positions as midshipmen. The board of officers from which he asked recommendations as to the scheme reported that in its judgment the rank of naval cadet should be created inferior to midshipman and all students should hold this until they went to sea on graduation. This corresponded to the status of a cadet at West Point, but the suggestion was not adopted and only from 1882 to 1902 was this the official title for a student at the Naval Academy.

The chief problem for Secretary Bancroft, after securing some support from the officers of the Navy for his idea, was how to set such a school going without asking Congress for a special appropriation and thus seeking its permission. This he accomplished by securing the transfer of Fort Severn from the War Department and by placing on waiting orders, where they would receive no pay, all the so-called "schoolmasters" formerly employed on board ship and at the various naval stations. The few retained were sent to Annapolis to join several naval officers from the regular list as instructors. As the students were simply midshipmen already on the payroll there were no additional expenses.

The command of this interesting experiment in naval education was given to Commander Franklin Buchanan, an officer of thirty years' service, one who had served several commands at sea and who was known as an efficient executive. The executive officer was Lieut. James H. Ward, who had been teaching at the Naval Asylum and had made a reputation as an instructor in gunnery and naval tactics. Professor Henry H. Lockwood, an ex-army officer, also came from Philadelphia to teach natural philosophy and, as it proved, introduce the midshipmen to infantry drill. Last, but not least in influence upon the school, was Professor William Chauvenet, who had graduated from Yale in 1840 and had in his few years in Philadelphia as a professor of mathematics in the Navy made his mark as a brilliant teacher, mathematician, and astronomer. These four men were the backbone of the institution and had more to do to make its early years successful than any others.

As late as the summer of 1845 it was only rumor in Annapolis that a naval school was to be established there, and not till August did a board of officers officially approve its location in the town, influenced apparently by Commodore Mayo, one of the board, who was an Annapolitan. On August 15th the formal transfer of Fort Severn was made, and on October 10th Commander Buchanan, with a staff of eight officers, assembled the forty-odd midshipmen who had reported in Annapolis and inaugurated the work of naval instruction. By the 18th the *Maryland Republican,* the successor of the old *Gazette,* had commented on the rapidity with which the change was being effected and remarked on the "forty young gentlemen whose handsome appearance and gentlemanly deportment give a cheerful aspect to the streets of our quiet city." [1]

The course of study reads as if it were very formidable, with its mention of arithmetic, algebra, geometry, navigation, geography, English grammar and composition, French, Spanish, trigonometry, astronomy, mechanics, optics, magnetism, electricity, ordnance, gunnery, the use of steam, history, natural philosophy, chemistry, infantry drill, and fencing, but the work was necessarily elementary, as the students had little preparation and were at all stages of attainment. The chief work of the first year

---

[1] One incident that broke the calm of the "quiet city" is related by no less a "character" than P. T. Barnum, the celebrated showman, in his autobiography. In 1836 he was a partner in a travelling circus that visited Annapolis. On the Sunday morning following his arrival, Barnum rather proudly donned a new black suit he had just purchased and sallied forth to see the town. Unfortunately in passing through the barroom he was seen by his partner Turner, an addict to practical jokes, who immediately started a rumor that the black-coated, ministerial-looking individual was a notorious clergyman from Rhode Island who had recently been the object of public indignation on account of his connection with the murder of a factory girl.

Consequently Barnum found a crowd following him, and was soon stopped and threatened with violence and a ride on a rail. When he learned the reason, he persuaded the mob to return with him to the hotel, where his partner laughingly admitted "he believed there was some mistake about it." In fact, the whole episode was a scheme of Turner's to increase the audience at the circus performances the next day.

was to prepare for examination those students who were due for promotion. The age of entrance was from thirteen to sixteen years, and the only admission requirement mentally was ability to read and write and some knowledge of arithmetic and geography.

No sooner had the Academy got into running order than the Mexican War opened and threw all into confusion. Midshipmen were detached for active duty, and even Buchanan himself left for a post at sea. The difficulty of adapting instruction and discipline to two very different classes, midshipmen who had made several cruises at sea, for the earliest students had entered the Navy as long before as 1840 and were thus quite mature in experience, and the class of youths who had just received papers as acting midshipmen and had had no experience on board ship, brought about various changes until 1851, when the four years' course was established substantially as at present. Thus the institution became a unit and not a place for haphazard cramming for examinations.

The atmosphere of the Academy during the

first fifteen years that followed its foundation and preceded the Civil War is well reflected in the recollections of those of its graduates who in later life wrote down their experiences, chiefly Alfred T. Mahan, the historian of sea power, who was a midshipman from 1856 to '59 and has left his record in "From Sail to Steam," his substitute for autobiography. Before him came several officers who distinguished themselves in junior commands during the Civil War, namely George H. Perkins and George Dewey.

Perkins, a New Hampshire youth, entered in 1851 and was so full of life and spirits and so little inclined to study that he was compelled to remain an extra year and not graduate till 1856. He had already, however, shown ability in target practice, and when he found himself under Farragut at New Orleans he piloted the swift gunboat *Cayuga* by the forts and against the Confederate steamers that were stationed farther up stream. Again at Mobile Bay he was in command of the monitor *Chickasaw* and delivered such a persistent fire of 15-inch shot against the stern of the Confederate ironclad

*From an etching by E. P. Metour, by permission of
E. H. Curlander, Art Dealer, Baltimore*

IN NEED OF REPAIRS

ram *Tennessee* that she was obliged to surrender to avoid being shot to pieces.[1]

Admiral Dewey's coming to Annapolis was, as he relates in his "Autobiography," somewhat of an accident, as he wished to go to West Point, but found the only appointment available was to the Naval Academy. He entered in 1854 at the age of fifteen years and eleven months, and after having been declared in his first year unsatisfactory in conduct, geography, and history, was saved to the Navy by a good record in mathematics, a more important subject than the last two. Dewey impressed his classmates as a likable lad, with marked refinement and natural dignity, and he rapidly progressed in class standing and in his influence upon his comrades. Generally known as "Shang" Dewey, he foreshadowed his future success and graduated fifth in his class. His poorest work at graduation had been in naval tactics and gunnery!

The one prank which is recorded against Dewey was a fist fight with another midshipman who called him some insulting name at the mess

[1] C. S. Alden, "George Hamilton Perkins," pp. 16-36.

table. They fought it out right there and were promptly haled before the Superintendent for punishment. The latter individual, however, declared that Dewey was justified in his action but imposed demerits as a punishment just the same.

At his very entrance to the Navy, Admiral Mahan gave also indications of his superior intellectual gifts. Having already had over a year at Columbia College, he did what no one had apparently thought of doing before and asked to be examined for entrance to the class which had already been in Annapolis one year. His success in securing this enabled him to graduate in three years. One of the aspects of the life of the Academy in his day was, as he looked back upon it in later years, the elevating social atmosphere which Annapolis possessed. As he remarks, "The phrase 'all sorts and conditions of men' never had wider or juster application than to the assembly of green lads, from every variety of parentage and previous surroundings, pitchforked into Annapolis once every year; and, of all the humanizing and harmonizing influences under which they came, none exceeded that of the quiet gentlefolk of moderate means with whom they mingled freely."

Mahan's career at the Naval Academy seems to have been uneventful, as was that of Commodore Winfield Scott Schley, who graduated in 1860. By this time the institution had thoroughly justified its existence and it had outgrown its quarters. In Dewey's time the midshipmen numbered about a hundred in all but in 1860 there were 281 at the beginning of the school year. Accordingly the entering class were quartered upon the *Constitution* which had been brought to Annapolis by David D. Porter.

This class numbering at entrance 100 was destined to take as active part in the naval activities of the next five years on both the Union and Confederate sides as any similar group. It has been called by one of its members, James M. Morgan, whose "Recollections of a Rebel Reefer" is a fascinating account of midshipman experiences during the Civil War, the "Brood of the Constitution." The officer in charge of the ship at that time was George W. Rodgers, who before the war ended met an heroic death in an assault on Fort Sumter in Charleston harbor.

Members of the class were in almost every major action of the naval forces during the war. In the fighting at Hampton Roads which culminated in the *Monitor-Merrimac* engagement, three of the class, Brown of Virginia, Carroll of Maryland, and Goode of South Carolina, were on the Confederate steamer, *Patrick Henry,* which assisted in destroying the wooden ships of the North. Peters of Tennessee was among the Confederates captured at Roanoke Island, and Long of Alabama was a midshipman on the *Merrimac* itself. Especially on the ironclad rams that made so many gallant attacks on the Union blockading ships and the river patrols were the Southern members of the class present. Long fought on the *Albermarle* when she damaged several Union gunboats at the mouth of the Roanoke River in 1863, Goode was attached to the ram, *Fredericksburg,* which was built at Richmond, as was also Meyer of Louisiana. Sevier of Tennessee served on the *Palmetto State,* which operated in Charleston harbor, Wilkinson joined the *Stonewall* on its cruise from Europe to Cuba, where it learned the war was over, and Peters of Tennessee was

Fort Severn 259

on board the *Atlanta* when a 15-inch shot from the rifled gun of the Union monitor *Weehawken* put it *hors de combat*. And at Mobile Bay and Fort Fisher other members who had joined the Southern ranks saw desperate service.

Practically all the class who remained true to the Federal cause were engaged on board the blockading fleet, on ships in the Mississippi, or in distant seas looking for Confederate raiders such as the *Alabama* or the *Florida*. And in the Spanish-American War, graduates from this class had probably a majority of the commands of fighting ships. Three of Dewey's captains were from them, Gridley of the *Olympia*, Coghlan of the *Raleigh*, and Wildes of the *Boston*. At Santiago Cook commanded the *Brooklyn*, Clark the *Oregon*, Evans the *Iowa*, and Taylor the *Indiana*—all entrants of this year. Admiral Sampson himself had graduated in 1860.

With the coming of the first rumors of secession there came a time which parallels strangely the period from 1775 to 1776 when before in Annapolis two parties gradually formed, those who stood for loyalty and those who stood for rebellion. And again there was displayed as nowhere else a kindly personal feeling between the two sides which is not often commented upon. The midshipmen had been together too long and had formed too close friendships to allow partisan feeling to overcome personal regard and affection. This was strikingly shown early in 1861, when an honor man of the graduating class resigned to follow his State, Alabama.

As Park Benjamin describes it in his collection of Annapolis traditions entitled "The United States Naval Academy,"

"The entire first class gathered and marched solemnly, with Acting Midshipman William T. Sampson—the other honor man—in the lead and arm in arm with the departing member, past the quarters and so on to the walk which ran in front of the officers' houses to the gate, singing in chorus a farewell song. As they came in front of the commandant's house, Lieutenant Rodgers suddenly appeared.

" 'What is the meaning of this rioting on Sunday night?' he demanded sharply.

" 'No riot, sir,' replied the leader; 'we are only bidding our classmate goodby.'

" 'Go on, gentlemen,' said the commandant simply, and the dreary little procession resumed its march."

As the various States seceded the boys from that State would send in their resignations as soon as they could get their parents' permission. In the case of Robley D. Evans, his mother, a Virginian, was more anxious for him to resign than he was himself and sent in his resignation for him. When Evans learned of it he had decided to stick by the North and after some difficulty got the action revoked by which it had been accepted. But after Sumter had been fired upon and Lincoln had called for troops the parting of the ways came definitely. Federal troops had arrived in Annapolis and the Academy was to be moved to Newport, R. I.

Accordingly when on the 24th of April Captain Blake, the superintendent, prepared to send the midshipmen away on the *Constitution,* the class of 1861 met and smoked together the pipe of peace, and pledged themselves to eternal friendship. When the drums beat for the final formation, all fell in as usual. Then C. P. R. Rodgers, the commandant, ordered the band to play "Hail Columbia" and "The Star Spangled Banner." With mixed emotions stirring in the breasts of the Southerners, he addressed the whole body with a fervent plea to stand by the old flag. Then, ceasing, he ordered those who wished to fall out to do so. The boys from the South who had followed their States and some from border States which had not left the Union stepped out of their places. Personal farewells followed, and many a boy from the North grasped the hand of his Southern friend or wound his arms about his neck while tears flowed freely. Then those who were to remain went aboard a tug to embark on the *Constitution,* while the rest walked resolutely out the gate into Annapolis on their way South.

CHAPTER XV

THE CIVIL WAR AND "BEN" BUTLER REACH ANNAPOLIS

EVEN before the departure of the *Constitution* with 151 midshipmen on board—the story of her departure has been only partially related—the critical situation of affairs at Annapolis had been in the mind of the superintendent. The town was thoroughly Southern in its sympathies, for Admiral Mahan says that he knew only one leading family that was really for the Union cause. Although Maryland had not seceded, there was considerable probability of her doing so, and in the event of hostilities breaking out it would be good policy for the Southern sympathizers to seize the Naval Academy with its guns and the frigate *Constitution* and thus close one approach to Washington to troops from the North.

Besides this, not all the officers at the Academy could be relied upon, and one in fact did resign as soon as Virginia seceded and there organized the Confederate Naval Academy. Accordingly we find Captain Blake writing to the Navy Department on the 15th of April in part as follows:

"The Department is probably aware that this point is not defensible against a superior force, and that the only force at my command consists of the students of the Academy, many of whom are little boys, and some of whom are citizens of the seceded States.

"If an attack should be threatened, with an exhibition of force stronger than we are able to repel, I propose to embark the officers and students in the school-ship *Constitution,* having first rendered useless the guns and ammunition which we may be compelled to leave on shore, and either defend her in this harbor, or if it be deemed more judicious, put to sea and proceed to New York or Philadelphia."

Gideon Welles, the Secretary of the Navy, replied approving the idea but warning against any premature movement that would precipitate matters. On the 20th, however, he telegraphed to Blake a message which in its incisiveness deserves to become historic. It read:

"Defend the *Constitution* at all hazards. If this cannot be done, destroy her."

The days were anxious ones for the aged superintendent, especially when he learned of the attack on the 6th Massachusetts as it passed through Baltimore on the 19th of April and heard the rumors that a crowd of Southern sympathizers were planning to take boat from there and seize the Naval Academy. But then came from an unexpected source assistance that removed all anxiety and placed the town in the firm possession of the Union forces.

This was no less than the arrival of the 8th Massachusetts under the command of Benjamin F. Butler and the 7th New York under its colonel. Probably there was not so much danger as Captain Blake feared but in Butler's colorful story of the affair, "Ben Butler's Book," as he called it, nothing that allowed a dramatic touch was omitted.

On account of the resistance to the passage of troops through Baltimore, Gen. Butler, who was at Philadelphia on the 19th, decided that some other route must be used to reach Washington. With characteristic independence, for he could not get in touch with the Massachusetts authorities or with the War Department, Butler decided to travel by railroad to Perryville on the northern bank of the Susquehanna, then take the steam ferryboat which had been used in transferring passengers across the river, and in it proceed to Annapolis, where he would be in railroad communication with the capital without touching Baltimore.

On the 20th he left Philadelphia and did not arrive off the harbor of Annapolis till nearly midnight. Much to his surprise, for he had not been able to send any word of his coming, he found the Naval Academy all lighted up and apparently expecting him.

Both parties, Butler and Blake, accordingly feared an attack, Blake that the steamer was from Baltimore with Southern partisans, and Butler that the place had already been captured for the South. According to "Fighting Bob" Evans, a midshipman at the time, general quarters was at once sounded on the *Constitution,* and the four 32-pounders which she had on board run out at her stern so as to command the approaching vessel. All the gun crews were at their stations when Rodgers on the *Constitution* hailed with:

"Ship ahoy! What ship is that?"

The reply was even more hostile,

"Ship ahoy! Keep off, or I will sink you."

Just then a voice which all on the *Constitution* recognized was heard,

"For God's sake, don't fire; we are friends."

It was the chaplain, who had been on leave and was returning with Butler.

When Captain Blake came on board Butler's vessel the next morning and was assured that rescue had arrived, he burst into tears, as Butler relates, and exclaimed:

"Thank God! thank God! Won't you save the *Constitution?*"

Butler, who knew more about politics than about the Navy, thought he referred to the Constitution as a document and replied,

"Yes, that is just what I am here for," but soon learned that he referred to the vessel, which was aground at its moorings and had too small a crew to make sail and get it out of the harbor. At once he again came to the rescue, with characteristic ardor, and said,

"Oh, well, I have plenty of sailor men from the town of Marblehead, where their fathers built the *Constitution*."

The fact that the ship had been built in Boston seems to have been passed over in the assurance of safety he gave.

Governor Hicks of Maryland vigorously protested against Butler's plan to land troops and proceed through the town to take train to Washington. He alleged that the excitement in the city was intense and the passage of troops sure to cause trouble. But Butler replied that he was without supplies for the journey to the capital by water and at once put his troops ashore. To protect the disembarkation and to prevent any possible assault on the Academy the midshipmen were landed under arms from the *Constitution* and remained all day deployed near the gate of the Academy. Admiral Evans gives his recollections thus:

"We stood in this position till the last soldier was ashore and the regiment had formed in line in rear of the midshipmen's quarters and stacked arms, when sentries from one battalion were posted and the rest of us returned to our quarters. Not a shot had been fired by either side, though the excitement was intense, and there was a readiness on both sides to fight. Both parties hesitated to fire the first shot, and the Confederates contented themselves with pitching stones over the wall, which we caught and tossed back. The newspapers gave graphic accounts of how Butler and his men had recaptured the Naval Academy! They never fired a shot nor saw a rebel to shoot at. The magazines of the *Constitution* were mined and she and her crew would have been blown to atoms before surrendering, if the rebels had attacked her." [1]

When Butler found that some of the railroad outside the town had had the rails torn up and thus rendered impassible, he sent out a force to seize the road and guard it during the reconstruction. He tells the story that when his men broke into a locked building and found there a small rusty locomotive, partly dismantled, he turned to the soldiers who accompanied him and asked,

"Do any of you know anything about such a machine as this?"

[1] R. D. Evans, "A Sailor's Log," p. 41.

One of them, Charles Homans, immediately stepped forward, took a good look at the engine, and replied,

"That engine was made in our shop; I guess I can fit her up and run her."

As soon as the road was open, Butler sent on the 7th New York and the 8th Massachusetts but remained behind in command of other troops which had arrived. On the 23d Butler and Hicks exchanged the following rather spicy correspondence:

"State of Maryland, Executive Chamber,
Annapolis, Maryland,
April 23, 1861.

To Brigadier General B. F. Butler:

Sir: Having, in pursuance of the power invested in me by the constitution of Maryland, summoned the Legislature of the State to assemble on Friday, the 26th instant, and Annapolis being the place in which, according to law, it must assemble; and having been credibly informed that you have taken military possession of the Annapolis and Elk-Ridge Railroad, I deem it my duty to protest against this step— because without at present assigning any other

reason, I am informed that such occupation of said road will prevent the members of the Legislature from reaching this city.
    Very Respectfully Yours,
        THOMAS H. HICKS."

"Headquarters, Third Brigade, U. States Militia,
    Annapolis, Maryland,
      April 23d, 1861.
To His Excellency Thomas H. Hicks, Governor of Maryland.

Sir: You were credibly informed that I have taken possession of the Annapolis and Elk-Ridge Railroad. It might have escaped your notice, but at the official meeting which was had between Your Excellency and the Mayor of Annapolis and the Committee of the Government and myself, as to my landing of troops, it was expressly stated as the reason why I should not land that my troops could not pass the Railroad because the Company had taken up the rails, and they were private property. It is difficult to see how it could be that if my troops could not pass over the Railroad one way the members of the Legislature could pass the other way. I have taken possession for the purpose of preventing the carrying out of the threats of the mob as officially represented to me by the Master of Transportation of the Railroad of this city, 'that if my troops passed over the Railroad the Railroad should be destroyed.'

. . . .

"I am endeavoring to save and not to destroy, to obtain means of transportation so I can vacate the capital prior to the sitting of the Legislature, and not to be under the painful necessity of encumbering your beautiful city while the Legislature is in session. I have the honor to be,

   Your Obdt. Servt.,
    BENJ. F. BUTLER,
     Brig. Genl. Comdg."

As a result of this dispute the Governor changed the meeting place to Frederick. But Butler asserts in his account that he warned the Governor that he would tolerate no discussion of secession, and the Governor reassured him on that point and even entrusted the Great Seal of the State to his keeping so that there would

The Civil War and "Ben" Butler

be no chance of its being affixed to an ordinance of secession.

One service must be credited to the fiery Yankee, though his shrewdness showed itself in the offer. According to Butler, Hicks was very much afraid of an uprising of the slaves, especially if the troops started to march through the State. Butler at once seized the opportunity to emphasize his position on the slavery question. He assured the Governor in a letter that he was not there to incite insurrection and would gladly co-operate in suppressing any such uprising. His forces, he stated, were at the Governor's disposal to act immediately for the preservation of the good order of the community.

The offer, however, got him into hot water with the Massachusetts authorities, to whom he was still subject. But to a reprimand from Governor Andrew, Butler replied with his accustomed energy:

"I had promised to put down a white mob and to preserve and enforce the laws against that. Ought I to allow a black one any preference in the breach of the laws? . . . The question seemed to me to be neither military nor political, and was not to be so treated. It was simply a question of good faith and honesty of purpose. The benign effect of my course was instantly seen. The good but timid people of Annapolis, who had fled from their houses at our approach, immediately returned; business resumed its accustomed channels; quiet and order prevailed in the city; confidence took the place of distrust, friendship of enmity, brotherly kindness of sectional hate, and I believe to-day there is no city in the Union more loyal than the city of Annapolis."

Butler remained in command at Annapolis till about the middle of May, during which time he sent a party to Frederick and arrested Ross Winans, Baltimore's richest citizen, and brought him to Annapolis, and also executed a dramatic "capture" of Federal Hill, Baltimore, during a terrific thunder storm, but he was soon transferred to Fortress Monroe, where he again attracted public notice by his decision that slaves were "contraband of war." Annapolis was used as the point of mobilization for the expeditions against Port Royal and Roanoke Island as far as troops were concerned, but otherwise it was chiefly a place for wounded men, who occupied the grounds and buildings at the Naval Academy and St. John's College, and as a reception point for prisoners. At first the grounds behind St. John's were used but later they were removed to what has since then been known as Camp Parole, three miles west of the town. At one time early in 1862 the authorities feared an attack from the Confederate ironclad battery, *Merrimac,* and made plans to board her with a large force of men and capture her by sheer weight of numbers. But she, of course, never arrived.

CHAPTER XVI

SINCE THE CIVIL WAR

WITH the close of hostilities between the North and South and the departure from Annapolis of Federal troops and wounded, the Naval Academy was enabled to return and reoccupy its quarters, sadly wrecked by their use as hospitals and by the erection of cheap, unsightly buildings for minor purposes, even for beer saloons. Almost immediately David D. Porter was assigned to the superintendency and in the course of his four years in office reconstructed both the external appearance and the internal organization of the institution.

Porter's career had been such as to stir the ambitions and fire the imaginations of the young men under him. A son of the famous David Porter of *Essex* fame, he had himself begun his naval experiences at the age of eleven on board a ship fighting pirates in the West Indies. When his father resigned from the American Navy and became for a short while a Mexican admiral, the son donned the uniform of a midshipman in the Mexican navy, but later enrolled as a midshipman in the navy of the United States. Although only a lieutenant at the outbreak of the Civil War, he became a rear admiral in less than two years, largely for his work on the Mississippi under Farragut, and he had full command in the closing days of the war of the attack on Fort Fisher, where the largest Union fleet assembled during the war, sixty vessels, was present. Four times he had been given votes of thanks by Congress.

Porter's energy and self-confidence found plenty of scope in the post he occupied. The Civil War had revolutionized the world's ideas of naval warfare, and steam engineering was at once given a prominent place in the curriculum. But Porter also changed the general character of the Academy from a school for mere boys to that of a college for men. He paid less attention to minor matters of conduct and encouraged athletic sports, especially baseball and rowing, and gave the midshipmen greater opportunities for social festivities and even such new ideas as amateur dramatics. During his time also appeared Park Benjamin's sketches of midshipman life, practically a class publication, entitled "Shakings."

As illustrating the new attitude of the superintendent to the midshipmen, is the story of Porter, then a Vice Admiral, putting on the boxing gloves and getting his nose smartly tapped by his midshipman opponent. But the older traditions of naval administration came back with the arrival of Commodore John L. Worden in 1869, although he had in the Civil War been the commander of the *Monitor* in its epoch-making engagement with the *Merrimac* under the command of Franklin Buchanan, the Academy's first head.

One of the interesting incidents of Naval Academy history in this period is the presence at the Academy of several famous ships. The *Constitution* has already been mentioned as arriving in 1860 as a practice ship, and after having served as quarters at Newport during the war she started back with the midshipmen on board. Though originally in tow of a tug, she broke loose and made the rest of the trip under her own sails, at times with a speed as great as thirteen and a half knots. From 1867 till 1871 she remained at her moorings, part of the time commanded by Lieutenant George Dewey, and serving as quarters for the entering class. Since her removal in '71 there has been an insistent demand by friends of the Academy that she should be returned to serve as a source of inspiration to the young men preparing for a naval life.

The other practice ship which remained at Annapolis for many years was the *Macedonian,* named for the British frigate captured by Decatur during the War of 1812 and often, though mistakenly, identified with her. She was first used by midshipmen in 1863 when they made a summer practice cruise to Europe in her. As American commerce was then being threatened by the activities of the Confederate cruisers, *Alabama* and *Florida,* Lieutenant Commander Luce, her commander, disguised her as a Spanish frigate and cruised all summer about the Bay of Biscay looking for Confederate raiders. The next summer she was again at sea with the midshipmen on a similar errand and the tradition is that one night off Block Island she actually had the *Florida* under her guns but burned a signal light too soon and so lost her quarry. She was used as late as 1868 for practice cruises.

Other ships with records of achievement which were sent to the Academy for varying periods were the *Constellation,* built in Baltimore in 1796, the same year as the *Constitution,* the *Hartford,* flagship of Farragut at both New Orleans and Mobile Bay, and the *Olympia,* from which Dewey directed the annihilation of the Spanish at Manila on the 1st of May, 1898. Lastly, the yacht *America,* which gave its name to the America Cup races, has a connection with Annapolis which has justified bringing the old craft there in recent years and preserving it in dignified surroundings. After winning the Queen's Cup, as it was then called, at Cowes in 1851 and thus establishing America's skill in sailing, she passed into British possession till she was sold to the Confederates in 1861 for blockade running. Her crew scuttled her in 1862 up the St. John's River, Florida, when they were pursued by the gunboat *Ottawa.* But she was soon raised and served off Charleston as a despatch boat. When her case came before the prize court her captors gave up all claim to prize money on condition that the Government would fit her up as a practice ship for the midshipmen. She thus reached the Academy and was used on summer cruises for a number of years. In 1873 the Secretary of the Navy sold her for a small sum to our Civil War acquaintance in Annapolis, General Benjamin F. Butler. After lying in a dilapidated condition in Boston harbor for many years she was at last brought to Annapolis in 1921 and presented to the Naval Academy.

An evidence of the advances made by the United States in naval reputation, and of the Naval Academy as well, was the decision of the Japanese Government to send some of its young men to Annapolis for training. These began to come in 1869 and continued at intervals till 1887. Of the fifteen Japanese who entered, Sotokichi Uriu, of the Class of 1881, proved the most distinguished when he commanded one of the cruiser divisions in the battle of Tsushima in 1905 and assisted in the disastrous defeat of the Russian fleet.

No history of the life of the Academy since the times of the Civil War can be complete without some reference to hazing, a custom which apparently dated from Civil War days at Newport when the upper classes were mostly in active service and there were but few officers to carry on the work of discipline. It was also probably due to imitation of customs at colleges and West Point. According to Admiral Mahan and to most of the older officers, there was no hazing in the 50's, for the "oldsters"—those midshipmen who had been at the Academy longer or had even served on board ship before entering—adopted a friendly attitude toward the entering class. But in 1871 eleven midshipmen were expelled for the offense. A fresh outbreak occurring in May, 1874, in June Congress passed the so-called "hazing law," by which any midshipman found guilty of hazing was to be summarily dismissed by the superintendent. This made no distinction between the different kinds of hazing, whether cruel or ridiculous, physical or mental, but considered any unauthorized assumption of authority by one midshipman over another to be worthy of dismissal.

In the various measures devised to eradicate the practice, which the passage of the "hazing law" failed to effect, there has been a great vari-

MAHAN HALL, NAVAL ACADEMY

ety. Some superintendents have adopted the rather strict, police-like methods by which the ships themselves were governed. Others have persuaded classes in the Academy to pledge themselves not to carry on physical or brutal hazing, in some cases using threats if this was not done, in others offering concessions or privileges. In other cases there has been an emphasis on the obligation resting upon the upper classmen as petty and cadet officers to report all cases of hazing or any other breach of the regulations that came to their notice, for it has generally been agreed that hazing could not go on without the knowledge of the graduating class. In all cases the fact that any one guilty of hazing in the very strict sense of the word as defined by Congress can be punished only by dismissal has made it impossible to regard some offenses as pranks and others as criminal. The greatest stir over the matter was probably in 1906 following a fight between two midshipmen, Branch and Meriwether, from which Branch died.

As in other institutions of learning, hazing in recent years has tended to diminish because of the larger number of students, the greater interest in athletics, which sidetracks attention to inter-class conflicts, and the general broadening of outlook which students experience by greater freedom of movement and a chance to divert their surplus energy in other directions, such as student publications and dramatics.

That the Naval Academy was essentially sound was demonstrated by the conduct of its graduates in the Spanish-American War, the first war where its product was in entire command. The deeds of the leaders have been already mentioned. At the beginning of the war junior officers were too few for the needs of the Navy and the graduating class was sent to the fleet in April. Soon after, the class to graduate in 1899 secured permission to join their comrades, and even members of the two lower classes were permitted to see active duty if they wished. After the battle of Santiago Rear Admiral Cervera and seventy-eight other officers were brought to Annapolis and quartered on the Naval Academy grounds to await arrangements for exchange or the end of the war. The liberal treatment accorded them left many a tender feeling for the town in their minds.

In the new developments in naval warfare which began in America about 1880, the adoption of steel ships, nickel-steel armor, and the application of electric power to the operations on board ship, the graduates of the Academy showed their progressiveness. Chief, perhaps, should be mentioned Bradley A. Fiske. Entering in 1870, when considerable hazing was in vogue, his particular humiliation was, as soon as he heard, "Jim Fiske, strike your attitude," to immediately assume the appearance of an idiot. Fiske's contributions to the new science of naval warfare were the first use of electricity for training guns, an improved range finder, the gun director system, a stadimeter, and finally in 1911 the torpedo plane.

Of other graduates of the Academy who about this time brought credit to their *alma mater,* Admiral Mahan revolutionized the world's conception of the importance of sea power on the development of nations and served as the guide for much of the naval expansion in Germany and Japan. His "The Influence of Sea Power on History," published in 1890, has placed his name with the great historians of the nineteenth century. In physics, a graduate of the time of Fiske, Albert A. Michelson, who soon left the navy for civil life, was the first one to measure the velocity of light and to prepare the world for the principle of physical relativity.

Probably, however, the Academy graduate who has done the most for the town itself in recent years was Winston Churchill, Class of 1894, when, having left the navy upon graduation and pursued a literary career, he returned to Annapolis, lived in the Governor Paca house, and wrote "Richard Carvel." The book was an instant success and directed attention to Annapolis as a charming bit of Colonial life still undisturbed. The foreword, put into the mouth of Daniel Clapsaddle Carvel, supposed grandson of the hero, pictured the town almost as it was in 1899, and offended many of the townspeople. But the book itself probably helped to destroy the sort of place it described. Churchill wrote:

"The lively capital which once reflected the wit and fashion of Europe has fallen into decay. The silent streets no more echo with the rumble of coaches and gay chariots, and grass grows where busy merchants trod. Stately ball-rooms, where beauty once reigned, are cold and mildewed, and halls, where laughter rang, are silent. Time was when every wide-throated chimney poured forth its cloud of smoke, when every andiron held a generous log—andirons which are now gone to decorate Mr. Centennial's home in New York or lie with a tag in the window of some curio shop. The mantel, carved in delicate wreaths, is boarded up, and an unsightly stove mocks the gilded ceiling. Children romp in that room with the silver door knobs, where my master and his lady were wont to sit at cards in silk and brocade, while liveried blacks entered on tiptoe. No marble Cupids or tall Dianas fill the niches in the staircase, and the mahogany board, round which has been gathered many a famous toast and wit, is gone from the dining room.

"But Mr. Carvel's town house in Annapolis stands to-day, with its neighbours, a mournful relic of a glory that is past."

With the close of the Spanish-American War, however, a new movement began in Annapolis. The Navy had demonstrated its value to the country and the possession of islands far distant from the continental United States made an increase in naval strength necessary. This involved a larger number of midshipmen to supply the officers for such ships. The accommodations at Annapolis were already inadequate and dilapidated; some buildings were unsafe and all were unsuited for a modern institution of naval education. Accordingly an entirely new plant was decided upon by the authorities. The original impulse probably came from Col. Robert M. Thompson, of New York, a graduate of the Academy in 1868, and a member of the Board of Visitors in 1895. So much interested was he in the matter that he enlisted the services of Mr. Ernest Flagg, the architect, and secured from him a plan for an entirely new arrangement of buildings and even changes in the grounds as well. This was the plan by which in the course of the next ten years the new Academy was constructed.

Since the outlay would be extensive, the Academy officials bided their time and in 1898, when a few buildings became wholly untenantable, they asked Congress for only a million dollars for a boat house, power house, and armory, only

*From a copyrighted photograph by Pickering, Annapolis.
Reproduced by permission*

NAVAL ACADEMY CHAPEL—MAUSOLEUM OF PAUL JONES

one-half of the needed money to be appropriated in the following year. These structures were to fit in with the plans of Mr. Flagg. In the course of the years before 1910 most of the features of the plan were secured at a total cost of over $10,000,000. At the same time the number of appointments was increased so that in 1905 the midshipman body numbered 881. The Academy reached its highest enrollment in 1923 with 2,499 on its rolls.

In 1906 occurred a fitting climax to all the work of rebuilding and expansion. On the 24th of April the body of Paul Jones, the first American naval officer to stamp himself upon history, was landed at the Naval Academy in the presence of a fleet of American and French warships and a large assemblage including President Roosevelt. In 1911 the original lead coffin was enclosed in a handsome marble sarcophagus and given a permanent resting place in the crypt of the Academy chapel.

The story of the finding of the remains of Jones is almost as romantic as was his life. When he died in 1792 in Paris he was buried in a Protestant cemetery in the outskirts of the city and the location of the grave promptly forgotten. But in 1899 General Horace Porter, then American ambassador to France, became interested in discovering the grave. After nearly six years of investigation, ended finally by tunnelling through what had been the cemetery where it was found that the lead coffin in which he had been buried had been placed, the body was discovered. Though the lead coffin had lost any name plate and a pick had penetrated one point and allowed the alcohol in which the body was preserved to evaporate, the original remains were discovered and found to correspond in every detail to busts of Jones by Houdon and with accounts of his physical condition at the time of death.

In the search for Jones General Porter met the considerable expenses necessary but the French and American governments gave the sacred remains of the naval hero a fitting funeral journey to Annapolis. The casket was escorted to the railroad station in Paris by companies of both French and American sailors, and at Cherbourg placed on board the U. S. S. *Brooklyn* and brought to Annapolis, where on the anniversary of Jones's first great victory, that of the *Ranger* over the *Drake,* it was received on shore; to serve as a perpetual incentive to patriotism and that spirit of undaunted courage which has always marked the American naval officer.

APPENDIX I

PLAN FOR DESTROYING BRITISH FRIGATES BY MEANS OF FIRE-BOATS CONTROLLED FROM SHORE

I AM indebted to Mrs. Margaret Roberts Hodges, of Annapolis, Genealogical Investigator, for the following plan for hauling fire-boats across Maryland rivers and thus setting on fire British ships of war which ventured up them to harass the villages and towns. It was found among the papers in the Land Office in Annapolis; on the back was a well-executed pen-and-ink drawing of the "Liverpool Frigate," 28 guns, one of the small British ships which operated in the Delaware, Chesapeake, and off the Virginia capes in 1776 and 1777. The author of the plan is indicated by the indorsement, "Jeremiah Riley's Scheme to Burn Ships of War." Riley was from Upper Marlboro, for later in the year Col. Joshua Beall charged "Lieut. Jeremiah Riley" with insubordination and a courtmartial was ordered. The document here quoted is addressed:

"On the Service of the United Colonies
Stephen West, Esquire
of the Woodyard near
Upper Marlborough in
By Express   Maryland."

It is endorsed, "Sunday, 10 o'clock, 18 February, [1776] forwarded to the Committee of Correspondence at Marlborough—S. W.," also, "Sunday, 1 o'clock, 18

February, forwarded to The Honorable The Council of Safety at Annapolis—D. Crawford."

Stephen West was a prominent patriot, gunsmith, and merchant of Upper Marlborough, and Crawford was another merchant of the same place in whose warehouse many of the provincial records were stored when removed from Annapolis for fear of an attack on the town. The time was just previous to the arrival of the *Otter* off Annapolis (for which see page 163), and in fact the *Otter* was for a time mistaken for the *Liverpool*. The following is the plan:

"A plan [which], if put in execution, would keep any large vessel from coming up any of our rivers where the channel runs nigh shore. Lay an anchor on the far side of the channel with a block on the nigher side; with a rope through the block bring both ends to shore; then fasten one end through the keel of the flat [boat] under water at the head of the flat [boat]. Then take another rope through the keel at the stern under water; then put two rag bolts in her head, one above the other well cased with iron, the hole through the boat bigger than the bolt, to let it turn to the ship side, having the bolt some length through the boat with a good head to it.

"Now fill the boat with anything that will burn quick, with some tar in a tub, hot, set to fly on the ship's side when the boat strikes. Now have some hot tar put in the boat, set it on fire when the ship is so nigh that she can't turn out of our way, then set our boat arunning with twenty men holt of the rope, run the boat against the ship;—if she don't burn I will burn for her.

Appendix I

"Now at the same time have another large boat under her head on fire with a large arm on head and stern for to hold her fast. Now, if two would not be safe, three or four would be a small charge. Now if the boat runs too fast stop her with the stern rope, for you may put her back or forward as you please. Now have your rope through a block at the waterside; as your rope won't be seen there, you may run them as you please."

APPENDIX II

A LIST OF THE GOVERNORS OF MARYLAND FROM THE ESTABLISHMENT OF THE CAPITAL AT ANNAPOLIS TO 1809, WITH DATE OF BEGINNING OF TERM.

Royal Governors

- 1694 Sir Francis Nicholson.
- 1699 Nathaniel Blackiston.
- 1703 Thomas Tench, President of the Council, Acting Governor.
- 1704 John Seymour.
- 1709 Edward Lloyd, President of the Council, Acting Governor.
- 1714 John Hart.

Proprietary Governors

- 1715 John Hart.
- 1720 Charles Calvert.
- 1727 Benedict Leonard Calvert.
- 1732 Samuel Ogle.
- 1733 Charles, Lord Baltimore.
- 1735 Samuel Ogle.
- 1742 Thomas Bladen.
- 1747 Samuel Ogle.
- 1752 Benjamin Tasker, President of the Council, Acting Governor.
- 1753 Horatio Sharpe.
- 1769 Robert Eden.

Appendix II

Governors under Independence

1777	Thomas Johnson.
1779	Thomas Sim Lee.
1782	William Paca.
1785	William Smallwood.
1788	John Eager Howard.
1791	George Plater.
1792	Thomas Sim Lee.
1794	John H. Stone.
1797	John Henry.
1798	Benjamin Ogle.
1801	John Francis Mercer.
1803	Robert Bowie.
1806	Robert Wright.
1809	Edward Lloyd.

APPENDIX III

SUPERINTENDENTS OF THE UNITED STATES NAVAL ACADEMY WITH DATE OF BEGINNING OF TERM

1845	Commander Franklin Buchanan.
1847	Commander George P. Upshur.
1850	Commander Cornelius K. Stribling.
1853	Commander Louis M. Goldsborough.
1857	Captain George S. Blake.
1865	Rear Admiral David D. Porter.
1869	Commodore John L. Worden.
1874	Rear Admiral C. R. P. Rodgers.
1878	Commodore Foxhall A. Parker.
1879	Rear Admiral George B. Balch.
1881	Rear Admiral C. R. P. Rodgers.
1881	Captain Francis M. Ramsay.
1886	Commander William T. Sampson.
1890	Captain Robert L. Phythian.
1894	Captain Philip H. Cooper.
1898	Rear Admiral Frederick V. McNair.
1900	Commander Richard Wainwright.
1902	Captain Willard H. Brownson.
1905	Rear Admiral James H. Sands.
1907	Captain Charles J. Badger.
1909	Captain John M. Bowyer.
1911	Captain John H. Gibbons.

Appendix III

1914 Captain William F. Fullam.
1915 Captain Edward W. Eberle.
1919 Captain Archibald H. Scales.
1921 Rear Admiral Henry B. Wilson.
1925 Rear Admiral Louis M. Nulton.

INDEX

AND

Glossary of Historical Facts about Annapolis

(For streets see under "Streets")

A

Acadians, 44, 112-3.
Acton, 134.
———, Richard, 134.
Adams, John, 114.
Addison, Joseph, 6, 70, 72, 82.
Aikman, William, 84.
Alabama, 279.
———, Claims, 244.
Allen, Bennett, 100.
   Rector, St. Anne's, 1767-8.
Alleys and Lanes,
   Carroll Alley, 3.
   Chancery Lane, frontispiece.
All Hallows Church, 71
America, 280-1.
   Yacht used by N. A. on practice cruises, 1863-4, 1866.
America Cup races, 280.
Andrew, Gov. John A., 273.
Annapolis, *passim*.
   City of historic charm, 1-9; settlement, 10-25; Act establishing, 26; made capital, 26-41; geographical advantages, 30-50; plan of town, 31, 125, 228; charter, 39-40; development, 42-50; fashion in, 53, 54; clubs, 61-71; theaters, 72-82; literature, 82-90; Tories and their homes, 92-108; Signers and their homes, 109-124; other citizens before the Revolution, 124-135; French wars, 136-8; Stamp Act, 138-42; taxes on tea, 145-53; Peggy Stewart Tea Party, 147-53; Revolution, 154-90; contest in courtesy, 154-76; departure of Gov. Eden, 165-75; visit of Lafayette, 178-80; French troops, 177-80; French officers, 181-8; Washington's visits, 191-224; Washington

resigns commission, 214-224; after Revolution, 225-33; proposed as capital of U. S., 227; Annapolis, Convention of 1786, 228-9; St. John's College, 235-8; Fort Severn, 245-7; founding of Naval Academy, 245-53; outbreak of Civil War; during Civil War, 263-75; publication of "Richard Carvel," 286-7.
Annapolis, described, (1700) 41; (1708) 43; (1730) 83; (1770) 206-7, 209-10; (1782) 181, 182-3; (1796) 229-30; (1798) 239-40; (1811) 241-4; (1899) 286-7; (1925) 1-9.
———, hospitality, 5, 182-3, 229, 242, 244, 254.
———, origin of name, 23.
———, alleys, see "Alleys."
———, streets, see "Streets."
Annapolis, 198.
Annapolis, composite gunboat used by N. A. for practice cruise, 1899.
Anne Arundel County, 18, 23, 29, 42, 146.
——— ——— ——— Committee, 142.
——— ——— Town, 23, 26, 30.
Anne, Queen, 1, 3, 23, 37, 39.
"Antilon," 144.
Armand, Gen., 186.
Armory, Old State, 134, 233.
  Stood just southeast of State House; used for balls, Governor's Council, etc. Torn down.
Arnold, Benedict, 178.
Articles of Association, 161.
Arundel, Earl of, 23.
Assembly Rooms (Ball Room), 133.
Associators, 29.

B

Bacon, Rev. Thomas (1700-1768), 88.
Bacon's Laws of Maryland, 88.
Bailey, Vernon Howe, drawings by, see list of illustrations.
Ball Room, 133.
Balls, 60, 155.
Ball's, see "Taverns."
Baltimore, City, 165, 166, 167, 170, 175, 215, 274.
———, Lord, 10, 11, 14, 15, 16, 18, 22, 23, 27-30, 30, 33, 40, 43, 84, 94-5, 137, 175.
Bancroft, George (1800-91), 247-9.
  Secretary Navy, 1845-6.
——— Hall, 7; built 1900.

Barber, Dr. L., 18.
Barnard, Dr. Henry (1811-1900), 237.
Barnes, Mrs., 196.
———, Col. Ab., 196.
Barnum, P. T. (1810-1891), 252.
Baylis, Henry, 219.
"Beggars Opera," 72.
Belair, 96.
Benjamin, Park, 260, 273.
Bennett, Richard, 12, 14, 24.
Black, William, 57-60.
Blackiston, Gov. Nathaniel, 42.
Bladen, Ann, 95.
  Married Benjamin Tasker in 1716.
———, Thomas (1698-1780), 94-5, 236.
———, William (1670-1718), father of Ann and Thomas; buried in St. Anne's.
———'s Folly, 95, 126, 236.
Bladensburg, 186, 234.
Blake, Capt. George, 261, 264-7.
  Superintendent N. A., 1857-65.
Bloomsbury Square, 135.
Bordley House, 126-8, 244.
———, John Beale (1727-1804), 128-9.
———, Stephen (1709-1764), 46, 54, 117, 126-7.
——— ———, Letter by, 46-49.
———, Thomas (1683-1726), father of Stephen and John Beale, 126.
Boston, 86, 145, 147.
Boucher, Jonathan (1738-1804), 66, 68, 194-7, 201-9, 238.
  Rector, St. Anne's, 1770-2; married 1772.
———, "Reminiscences," 209.
———, Letters to Washington, 201-9.
Branch, J. R., Jr., 283.
  Midn. N. A., 1903-Nov. 7, 1905.
Brandywine Campaign, 177.
Bray, Thomas (1656-1730), 36-7.
Brice House, 4, 103-4.
———, James, 103.
Brogden, Rev. William, 71.
Brooke, Mr., 48.
Browne, Orris A., 258.
  Midn. N. A., 1860, from Va.
Bruce, Mrs., 239.

Buchanan, Comdr. Franklin (1800-74), 250-3, 278.
　Supt. N. A., 1845-7.
Bull Baiting, 56.
Burwell, Mr., 195.
Butler, Gen. Benjamin F., 9, 265-72, 281.

C

Calvert, Benedict Leonard, 83.
———, Eleanor, 208.
———, Leonard, 10, 24.
———, Mr., 208.
Camden, Lord, 142.
Camp Parole, 275.
Canterbury, Archbishop of, 34.
"Carmen Seculare," 84.
Carroll, Charles (1660-1720), 110-1.
———, Charles, of Annapolis (1702-82), 111-3.
———, Charles, of Carrollton (1737-1832), 109-16, 143, 152, 159, 187, 196, 219, 225, 235.
———, Charles, Barrister (1723-83), 132-3, 135, 162, 166-7, 170, 194, 225.
———, Charles, Doctor (d. 1755, age 64), father of Barrister.
——— House, 111-2.
———, Rev. John (1735-1815), 116, 235.
———, William Joseph, 258.
　Midn. N. A., 1860, from Arkansas.
Carvel Hall Hotel, 117-8.
Carvel, Richard, 4, 7, 102, 105.
Catholics, 11, 34, 36, 105, 110, 112-3, 144, 235.
"Cato," 72.
Caton's Barber Shop, see "Houses."
Cervera, Adm. Pascual, 284.
Chambrun, Marquis de, 190.
Charles I, 10, 27.
——— II, 22.
Chase House, 119-24, 238.
———, Jeremiah T., 224, 242.
———, Mrs. J. T., 242.
———, Miss, 242.
———, Samuel (1741-1811), 116, 119-24, 131, 145, 155, 159, 162, 219, 225, 233, 235.
　Vestryman, St. Anne's, 1770-2, 1775-7, 1779.

Chauvenet, Prof. William (1820-70), 251.
   Prof. Mathematics and Navigation, N. A., 1845-59.
Chesapeake, 7, 246.
Chesapeake, sailing ship used by N. A. for practice cruises, 1900-1.
Chestertown, 76, 192, 198.
Chew, Family, 128.
——, Mary, 117.
Chimney sweeps, 3.
Churchill, Winston (1871 —), 7, 102, 105, 117-8, 286-7.
   Midn. N. A., 1890-4; resigned 1894.
City Hotel, see "Taverns."
Civil War, 237, 257-75.
Claggett, Rev. Thomas J., 235.
Claiborne, William, 14.
Clapham, J., 66-7.
Clark, Capt. Charles E. (1843-1922), 259.
   Midn. N. A., 1860-3; instr. N. A., 1870-3.
Clemens, Samuel C. (Mark Twain), visited Annapolis and lectured in State House in 1906.
Clinton, Vice-Pres. George (1739-1812), 223.
Clubs, 55, 61-71, 84, 195.
   Conundrums, 64; Drumstick, 70; Gelastic Law, 63; Homony, 66-9; Independent, 70; Jockey, 55, 195; Mock trials, 62; Tuesday, 61-6, 84; Two-Penny, 70; Ugly, 70.
Coaches, vehicles, 55, 97.
Cock fighting, 56.
Coffee House, see "Taverns."
Coghlan, Capt. Joseph B. (1844-1908), 259.
   Midn. N. A., 1860-3.
Cole, Charles (d. 1757), 64.
Committee of Correspondence, 119, 133.
"Considerations," Dulany's, 98-9, 140-2.
Constellation, frigate, built Baltimore, 1794-6; used by N. A. for practice cruises, 1871-93.
Constitution, frigate, 241, 257, 262-8, 278-9.
   Built Boston, 1794-6; used by N. A., 1860-1871.
Continental Congress, 79, 114, 118, 155, 167, 171-2, 214-24, 226-8.
Convention, Maryland, 155-6, 159-60, 169-72.
Convicts, 45.
Coode, John, 29.
Cook, Ebenezer, 42-3, 82-3.

Cook, Capt. Francis A. (1843-1916), 259.
   Midn. N. A., 1860-3; instr., 1868-70, 1879-83.
   ———, Master, 20.
Copley, Sir Lionel, 29, 30.
Corson, Prof. Hiram, 237.
Council House, 32, 48.
   ——— Room, 47, 59.
Council of Safety, 161, 165-74.
County Party, 120, 137.
Coursey, Henry, 18.
Court Party, 61, 137, 141, 144.
Court of Pypowdry, 40.
Craik, Dr. James, 196.
   ———, John, 196.
Cromwell, 13, 15.
Cushing, William B. (1842-74), Midn. N. A., 1857-61; resigned 1861.
Custis, George Washington Parke, 238-41.
   ———, John Parke, 195-208.
   ———, Miss, 196.

D

Dahlgren Hall, Naval Academy, named for Rear Adm. John A. Dahlgren (1809-1870), instr. gunnery N. A., 1848; ordnance expert and inventor of Dahlgren gun.
Dale, sailing ship, stationed at N. A. and used on practice cruises, 1867-9, 1880-4.
Dartmouth College Case, 236.
Declaration of Independence, 109, 116-20.
Declaration of Rights, 133, 156-8.
De Closen, Baron Jean (b. 1752), 182-3.
De Grasse, Comte, 180.
Delaware, 24.
Dewey, Commodore George (1837-1907), 255-9, 279-80.
   Midn. N. A., 1854-8; instr. N. A., 1867-70.
Dickinson, John (1732-1808), 88, 142, 228.
   ——— ———, "Letters of a Pennsylvania Farmer," 142.
Digges, Ignatius, 194, 198.
   ———, William, 194.
"Don't Give Up the Ship," flag, 7.
Dorsey, Maj. Edward, 30.
   ——— House, 30.
Dougheregan Manor, 110-11.

Duff, Simon (d. 1759, age 59), 101.
  Vestryman, St. Anne's, 1744.
Dulany, Ann, 184-6.
———, Daniel, Elder (1685-1753), 97-9.
  In Annapolis, 1721-53; buried in St. Anne's.
———, Daniel, Younger (1722-97), 88, 97-9, 140-4, 194, 197, 207.
  Married Rebecca Tasker, 1747; buried in Baltimore.
  ——— House, 99-100.
———, Kitty (Mrs. Belt), 187-8.
———, Lloyd (1742-82), 99-100, 194, 197.
Dulany, M [ary Grafton], 187-8.
———, Walter (son of Daniel, Elder; d. 1773), 99, 100, 187, 247.
———, Walter (son of Walter), 187.
Dunmore, Lord, 160.
Durand, William, 13.
Dustin, Hannah, 38.
Dutch, 24.
Duval, Mr., 242.

E

Eddis, William, 53, 66, 76, 81, 80-90, 145-7, 152, 161, 175, 213.
Eden, Sir Robert (1741-1784), 102, 105, 125, 143, 146-7, 159-76, 186, 194-8, 207, 210, 213.
Education, 33, 235-8.
Ellery, William, 218.
Eltonhead, William, 19.
England, politics affect Annapolis, 10, 13; visits to, 52; marriages with Englishmen, 52; imitation of, 52-6, 84; children sent to, for education, 98.
Enterprise, cruiser, stationed at N. A., 1891-2.
Episcopal church, 34-5, 144, 231-2.
Essex, frigate, 233, 276.
Evans, Capt. Robley D. (1846-1912), 259, 261, 266, 268-9.
  Midn. N. A., 1860-3; instr. 1872-4.

F

Faris's, see "Taverns."
Farragut Field, N. A., named for David D. Farragut (1801-1870); memorial window in Chapel.
Ferry over Severn, 31.
Fire engine; the "Victory," a fire engine, was purchased in 1755.

"First Citizen," 143.
Fiske, Rear Adm. Bradley A. (1854 —), 285.
   Midn. N. A., 1870-4.
Fitzhugh, Mr., 195.
Flagg, Ernest, 288-9.
Flags, captured, 7; Perry's, 7; Star Spangled Banner, 238.
Florida, cruiser, 279.
Foster, Abiel, 218.
Fowey, British frigate, 174.
Fox, George, 34.
France, 163.
Franklin, Benjamin, 63, 87, 115, 117, 193.
Franklin House, see John Shaw House.
French officers, 123.
Fuller, Capt. William, 16.

G

Gage, Gen. Thomas, 160.
Gale, Col., 49.
Galloway, Samuel, 194-6.
Garrett, Amos (d. 1727 in 56th year), 135.
   Tombstone in St. Anne's; see his curious will in Land Office, Annapolis, giving away a thousand books and many pairs of gloves. Vestryman, St. Anne's, 1704-20.
Garretson's, see "Taverns."
Gas, illuminating, first used in the town in 1859.
Gates, Gen. Horatio, 219.
———, Tom, 30.
Gerry, Elbridge, 218.
Golden Lion, 16-17, 19, 22.
Goode, W. W., 258.
   Midn. N. A., 1860-1.
Good Intent, 142.
Governor's Mansion, 27, 57, 101-3, 173.
   Present Governor's Mansion erected 1866 on site of house of Dr. George Stewart (q. v.).
Green, Anna Catherine, 87.
———, Jonas (1712-67), 63-5, 74-5, 86-8, 134, 234.
——— House, 134.
——— Street, opened by Dr. Charles Carroll in 1752.
Greene, Gen. Nathaniel, 177.
Greenberry Point, 13, 23-4.
Gridley, Capt. Charles V. (1845-98), 259.
   Midn. N. A., 1860-3; instr. N. A., 1875-9.
Guerriere, 7.

H

Hall, John, 166, 170.
Hamilton, Alexander (d. 1756), 61-6, 71, 84-5.
———, Alexander (1757-1804), 218, 228.
   Contributed $10 to St. John's in 1786.
Hammond, Maj. Gen. John (d. 1707), tombstone in St. Anne's; Bible bought by vestry with bequest of £10. Vestryman, 1704.
———, Philip (d. 1766), 134.
———, Matthias (d. 1786), 130, 144, 148.
Hardy, Samuel, 218.
Harris, Matthew, 46.
Hartford, screw sloop, 280.
   Built 1858; used by N. A. for practice cruises, 1903-9; stationed at N. A., 1906-12.
Harwood House, 129-31, 234.
Hawkins, Benjamin, 218.
Hazing, 281-4.
"Heamans' Narrative," 17.
Heamans, Roger, 16, 19, 22.
Hesselius, John, 91.
Hessians, 163.
Hicks, Gov. Thomas Hollyday, 268, 270-3.
Higginbotham, Rev. Ralph (d. 1813), 232.
   Rector, St. Anne's, 1774-1804; Master, King William's School, 1774-85; Prof. Languages, St. John's, 1789-1813; Vice Principal, 1792-1813.
Holdsworth, Edward, 84.
Hollyday, James (1727-1788), 162.
Homony Club. See "Clubs."
Hood, Zachariah, 138-40.
Hope, 179, 184.
Horses, race, 55-6, 87, 96, 193-9.
Houdon, 290.
Houses. Following is a list of the chief houses still standing in Annapolis which date from before the Revolution. See also "Taverns."
   Acton (q. v.).
   Aunt Lucy Smith's Bakeshop, 160 Prince George Street. Home of a famous colored cook.
   Bordley House (q. v.).
   Brice House (q. v.).
   Carroll House (q. v.).

Houses:
  Caton's Barber Shop, corner Fleet and Cornhill Streets. Here Washington is said to have been shaved by William Caton before the ceremony of resignation.
  Dorsey House (q. v.), 211 Prince George Street.
  Franklin House. Same as John Shaw House (q. v.).
  Green, Jonas, House (q. v.).
  Harwood House (q. v.).
  Jennings House (q. v.).
  Larkin House. On site, No. 139 Market Street, where in 1718 William Larkin is marked on Stoddert's survey as having his dwelling.
  McCubbin House, 193 Main Street, at one time a tavern.
  Ogle House (q. v.).
  Paca House (q. v.).
  Pinkney House (q. v.); see also p. 234.
  Randall House. See Bordley House.
  Reverdy Johnson House. See page 244.
  Ridout House (q. v.).
  St. Anne's Rectory, No. 217 Hanover Street. Sold in 1885. See St. Anne's.
  Sands House, No. 110 Prince George Street. Here Washington is said to have taken refuge from a crowd following him in 1783.
  Scott House (q. v.), sometimes called the Carvel House.
  Shaw House (q. v.).
  Sparks House, No. 179 Duke of Gloucester Street. History unknown.
  Stewart, Peggy, House, No. 207 Hanover Street (q. v.).
  Tilton House, No. 9 Maryland Avenue. History unknown.
Howell, David, 218.
Humphries, David, 219.
Humphreys Hall, St. John's College; erected 1835; named for Rev. Hector Humphreys (1797-1857), Pres. St. John's, 1831-57.
Hunter's, see "Taverns."
Hunting Ridge, 175.

I

Independent Club, see "Clubs."
Indians, 23-4, 29, 44, 57.
Irving, Washington, 62.
Isherwood Hall, Naval Academy; named for Engineer-in-Chief B. F. Isherwood, engineering expert.
"Itinerarium," Hamilton's, 85.

J

James II, 23, 27, 281.
Japanese at N. A., 281.
Java, 7.
Jefferson, Thomas, 200, 218, 223, 233.
Jenifer, Daniel of St. Thomas, 162, 194-8.
Jennings, Edmund (d. 1757), 57, 101-3.
——— House, 103-4.
———, Juliana, 103.
———, Thomas (d. 1759), 103-4.
Jockey Club, see "Clubs."
Johnson, Reverdy (1796-1876), 244.
    Grad. St. John's, 1811.
———, Thomas (1732-1819), 162-3, 197.
Johnson's, The Widow, see "Taverns."
Jole, Master, 64-5.
Jones, Paul, 7, 289-91.
Jusserand, Ambassador Jules, 181.

K

Kent Island, 14.
Key, Francis Scott (1779-1843), 238.
    At St. John's College, 1789-96.
King's College (Columbia), 208.
King William's School, 33-4, 84, 134, 235-6.

L

Lady Prevost, flag of, 7.
Lafayette, George Washington, 190.
Lafayette, Marquis de la, 178-82, 184, 189, 190.
Langford, John, 22.
Larkin, Thomas, see "Houses."
Lawrence Field, Naval Academy, named for James Lawrence (1781-1813); died after *Chesapeake-Shannon* engagement; dying words, "Don't give up the ship," 7.
Lee, Arthur (1740-92), 218.
———, Gen. Charles (1731-82), 166.
———, Jesse (1758-1816), 233.
———, Gov. Thomas Sim (d. 1819, age 75), 213.
Leggat, Mr., 19.
L'Emeraude, 187.
Lewis, Richard, 83.
———, William, 19.

Lexington, Battle of, 156.
Liberty Poplar, 25, 126, 233.
Libraries, 37, 84-5.
Literature, 82-90; poetry, 82-4, 244; printing press, 86-7; *Maryland Gazette*, 87-8.
Liverpool, British warship; see Appendix I.
Lloyd, Col. Edward (d. 1696), 22, 122.
——, Edward IV (1744-1796), 121, 129, 195, 218.
——, Gov. Edward V (1779-1834), 123, 243.
——, Madame, 182-3.
——, Mary Tayloe (1784-1859), 238.
——, Richard Bennett (1750-1787), 182-3.
Loan Office, 175.
Lockwood, Prof. Henry Hayes (1814-99), 250.
  Prof., Naval Asylum, 1841-5; N. A., 1845-61, 1866-71.
——, James Booth (son of H. H., 1852-84); born in Annapolis; Class of 1873, St. John's; died at Cape Sabine during Greely Polar Expedition; buried N. A. Cemetery.
Lomas, John (d. 1757), 71.
Long, James C., 258.
  Midn. N. A., 1859-61; appointed from Tennessee.
Loyalists, 92-108, 131-2, 156.
Luce, Lt. Comdr. Stephen B. (1827-1917), 279.
  Midn. date of 1841, at N. A., 1848; instr. and comdt., 1859, 1861-3, 1865-8.

M

Macdonough Hall, Naval Academy; named for Commodore Macdonough (1783-1825), victor at Lake Champlain, 1814.
Macedonian, frigate, 7.
——, American built frigate, 279.
  Used by N. A. for practice cruises, 1863-9.
Macpherson, Maj., 184.
Madison, James, 228, 233.
Mann, Mr., 215 (see also "Taverns").
Market, 134 (see also "Streets").
Mary, Queen, 27.
Maryland, 10, 192; royal province, 29; in Revolution, 177-82, 217-8; in Civil War, 263, 270-4.
Maryland Gazette, 63, 69-76, 78, 80, 84, 86-8, 140-3, 153, 156, 159, 209, 213, 251.
Maryland Republican, 251.

Mahan, Capt. Alfred T. (1840-1914), 254, 263, 282, 285-6.
   Midn. N. A., 1856-9; instr., 1862-3, 1877-80.
Mason, Mrs., 243.
Masons (fraternity), 71, 87.
Massachusetts, 8th Regiment, 265-7, 270.
Maury Hall, Naval Academy, named for Matthew Fontaine Maury (1806-73), officer in U. S. and Confederate navies, noted for investigations of winds and currents; early advocate of a naval academy.
Mayo, Commodore Isaac, 251.
   Born in Annapolis, entered Navy, 1809, dismissed 1861.
McCloud's, see "Taverns."
McComb, Eleazer, 218.
McCubbin, Mary, 133.
McDowell, Dr. John (d. 1821), 236, 238-9.
   Prof. Mathematics, St. John's, 1789; Principal, 1790-1807; McDowell Hall named for him about 1860.
McHard's, see "Taverns."
McHenry, Fort, 246.
McHenry, James, 218, 227.
McNeir, Thomas, 139.
Meriwether, M., Jr., 283.
   Midn. N. A., 1904-6.
Merrimac, 275.
Methodism, 232-3.
Metour, Eugene P., etcher, see List of Illustrations.
Mexican War, 253.
Meyer, Cassius, 258.
   Midn. N. A., 1860-1; appointed from Miss.
Michelson, Prof. A. A. (1852——), 286.
   Midn. N. A., 1869-73; resigned in 1881.
Middleton, Samuel, 71.
Middleton's, see "Taverns."
Midshipmen, early education, 248-9; education at Naval Academy, 250-3; in Mexican War, 253; in Civil War, 257-9; in Spanish-American War, 259, 284-5.
Mifflin, Gen. Thomas, 186, 216, 218, 220, 223.
Militia, 48-9, 155, 160.
Monitor-Merrimac, engagement, 258, 275, 278.
Monk, 179, 184.
Monongahela, sailing ship used for practice cruises by N. A., 1895, 1896, 1899.
Montague, Capt. George, 174.
Monroe, James, 218, 233.

Morgan, James M., 257.
Midn. N. A., 1860-1; appointed from La.
Morris, Cadwalader, 218.
Murray, Dr. James, 243.
"Muscipula," 84.

N

Nantucket, monitor, stationed at Naval Academy, 1876-80.
Naval Academy, described, 7; founding, 245-53; earlier instruction, 248-9; early days, 253-62; removal to Newport, 261; departure of Southerners, 261-2; danger of capture by South, 263-5; Butler arrives, 265-74; used as hospital, 275-6; after Civil War, 276-91; changes by Adm. Porter, 276-8; famous ships at, 278-81; Japanese at, 281; hazing, 281-4; in Spanish War, 284; famous graduates, 285-6; rebuilding, 287-9; burial of Paul Jones, 289-91; increase in enrolment, 289; chapel, 7, library, 103. Superintendent's house, 101.
Naval Asylum, 248-9.
Naval Cadet, 249.
Negroes, 44-9, 273-4.
Newport, R. I., 261, 278, 282.
New York, 153.
———, 7th Regiment, 265, 270.
Nicholson, Sir Francis (1660-1728), 30-3, 38, 40, 85.
———, Commodore James (1737-1804), 178-9.
Non-Importation, 142, 155.
Norfolk, 12.
Nuthead, Dinah, 86.

O

Ogle, Gov. Benjamin (1749-1809), 183, 198.
———, Mrs. Benjamin, 183-5.
———, House, 96.
———, Mary, 106-7.
———, Gov. Samuel (1694-1752), 55-6, 96, 183.
———, Mrs. Samuel, 224.
Olympia, cruiser, 280.
 Launched 1892; stationed at N. A., 1907-12; used by N. A. for practice cruises, 1907-9, 1922.
Osgood, Samuel, 218.
Otter, 163-4.

P

Paca, William (1740-99), 67, 116-9, 144, 155, 158-9, 166, 170, 219, 227, 235.
    Vestryman, St. Anne's, 1771-3.
——— House, 116-8, 286.
Packer, Mr., 18.
Painting, 90-1.
Parks, William, 43, 86.
Partridge, George, 218.
Peale, Charles Willson (1741-1827), 66, 81, 91.
Peggy Stewart, 130, 148, 154.
Peggy Stewart Tea Party, 147-53.
Pendleton, Mr., 195.
Perkins, Lt. George H. (1836-99), 254-5.
    Midn. N. A., 1851-6.
Perry, O. H., 7.
Peters, James A., 258.
    Midn. N. A., 1860-1; appointed from Tenn.
Phlox, steam tender in use at N. A. from about 1865 to 1891; commemorated in Phlox Landing.
Pinkney Hall, St. John's, built 1857, named for William Pinkney, diplomat.
Pinkney House, built by John Callahan, Clerk of Land Office; erected on present site of Court of Appeals Bldg.; removed to present site, 5 St. John's St., about 1905.
Pinkney, Ninian, 131, 234.
    Graduated, St. John's, 1793.
———, William, diplomat (1764-1820), 233-5, 243.
———, William, bishop, 131.
Piscataway Town, 197.
Piscataways, 24.
Pitt, William, 98, 141-2.
Plater, George, 97.
Pope, Alexander, 82, 84.
Pope's "Dunciad," 61.
Porter, Commodore David (1780-1843), 276-7.
———, Adm. David D. (1813-1891), 257, 276-8.
    Supt. N. A., 1865-9.
———, Gen. Horace, 290.
Portsmouth, N. H., 85.
Port Tobacco, 192.
Powder House, a small building near where the Scott House stands, 47.

Presbyterians, 34, 236.
Prince George's County, 46.
Princeton College, 238.
Printing, 85-8, 141.
Prison, Stoddert's map of 1718 shows site to be between West and Cathedral Streets and near their junction.
Proctor, Richard, 23.
Proctor's, 23, 26.
Proctor's Landing, 13, 26.
Providence (Annapolis), 13, 22-3.
Pryse, Thomas, 55.
Puritans, 10-25.
Purviance, Samuel, 166.

Q

Quakers, 34, 37-7, 43-4.

R

Railroad, 269-70.
  Railroad from Annapolis to B. & O. at Annapolis Junct. opened in 1840; direct line to Baltimore, over Severn River, opened in 1887; both electrified in 1908; service through streets of town begun in 1908.
Randall, D. R., 13n.
——— House (Bordley), 127.
Randolph, Edmund, 228.
———, Mr., 195.
Read, Jacob, 218.
Reina Mercedes, Spanish cruiser captured at Santiago on July 4, 1898; station ship at N. A., 1912 ———.
Religion, 11, 33, 35, 37, 231-2.
Reynolds, Sir Joshua, 183.
Reynolds's, see "Taverns."
"Rhapsody," 84.
"Richard Carvel," 4, 7, 105-6, 117, 286-7.
Ridout, Hester Anne Chase, 124.
——— House, 106-8.
——— Houses, 132.
———, John (1732-1797), 106-8, 124, 193-8, 210.
———, Mrs. John, 224.
———, Mary, 193.
Riley, Lieut. Jeremiah. See Appendix I.
Robin, Abbe, 181.
Rochambeau, Comte de, 178, 182, 187.

Rochefoucault-Liancourt, Count de, 229-30.
Rock Hall, 192, 198.
Rodgers, Adm. C. R. P. (1819-1892), 260-1.
　Comdt. N. A., 1860-61; supt., 1874-8, 1881.
——, Lt. George W., 257.
　Comdt. N. A., 1861-2.
Rogers, Col., 49.
Roosevelt, Theodore, 289.

S

St. Anne's, 2, 41, 71; founding, 35-6; communion silver, 37; growth, 50, rectory, 131; before Revolution, 134-5; Boucher, rector, 201-10; rebuilt, 231-2; present church built 1858.
St. John's College, 25, 37, 95, 180, 235-41, 275.
St. Margaret's Church, 175.
St. Mary's Church, 10, 15, 27, 30; site given in 1852; present church erected in 1858.
Sampson, Adm. William T. (1840-1902), 259-60.
　Midn. N. A., 1857-61; instr., 1862-3, 1869-71, 1875-9; supt., 1886-90; Sampson Hall named for him.
Sands House. See "Houses."
Santee, sailing sloop; keel laid in 1820, launched in 1855; school ship at Newport, 1862; station ship at N. A., 1865-1905; sank, 1912; burned for metal in Boston, 1913.
Savannah, screw steamer used by N. A. for practice cruises, 1866-70.
Schley, Commodore Winfield Scott (1831-1911), 257.
　Midn. N. A., 1856-60; instr. 1866-9, 1873-6, 1884; owned brick house cor. Cathedral and Franklin Sts.
School, 33, 41.
Schoolmasters, naval, 248, 250.
Scots, 62.
Scott, Dr. Upton (1722-1814), 85, 104-6, 175, 242-3; buried in St. Anne's Cemetery.
——, Mrs. Upton (d. 1819, age 80), 238.
　Married 1756; buried in St. Anne's Cemetery.
—— House, 104-6, 175, 238.
Sedan Chairs, 4, 55.
Selfridge, Thomas O., Jr. (1836-1924), first graduate of full course at N. A. Midn. 1851-4; instr., 1865-8.
Senate Chamber, 214-20.
Senecas, 24.

Servants, indentured, 44-5, 97, 149, 174.
Severn, 22-3, 177.
Severn, Battle of the, 15-22.
———, Fort, 101, 245-7, 249-51.
———, Heights, 175.
Sevier, Charles F., 258.
   Midn. N. A., 1860-1; appointed from Tenn
Seymour, Gov. John, 39.
Shakespeare, plays presented in Annapolis, 73, 75-6, 79-81.
Sharpe, Gov. Horatio (1718-1790), 102, 105-7, 124, 136-9, 146, 192, 197, 207, 210.
Shaw, Dr. John (1778-1809), 244.
——— House, 244.
Ship Tavern, see "Taverns."
Slavery, 44, 272-3.
Smallwood, Gen. William (1730?-1792), 219.
Smith, William S., 219.
Social Life, 5-6, 55-60, 96-7, 127, 181-3; balls, 194-9; cards, 194-200.
Sons of Liberty, 118, 139-40.
"Sot-Weed Factor," 42-3, 82-3.
"Sot-Weed Factor Redivivus," 83.
Spa Creek, 15.
Spaight, Richard Dobbs, 218.
Spanish-American War, 259, 284, 287.
Spectator, 70, 82.
Sprigg, Richard, 198.
   Lived at Strawberry Hill, now N. A. Golf Links.
Stamp Act, 102, 138-42.
State House, 1-2, 5, 27, 32, 41, 115, 125, 181, 214-23, 230.
Steele, Richard, 6, 70.
Stewart, Anthony, 131, 144, 148-54.
———, Dr. George, 194.
———, *Peggy*, House, 153.
   Built probably in 1763; now 207 Hanover St.
Stone, Thomas, 162, 219.
———, William, 11-21.
———, Virlinda, letter by, 18-21.
Streets, 3, 125.
   The following streets are named on the survey of Annapolis by James Stoddert in 1718 (copy in Mayor's Office) and are the same to-day, except as noted:
Bishop, same as Franklin, west of Cathedral.
Bladen, intersects Bloomsbury Square, named for William Bladen.

Streets, Bloomsbury Square, bounded by Northwest, Calvert, St. John's and College Ave.
Calvert.
Carroll.
Cathedral.
Charles.
Church, present Main St., ending at water's edge, where street to-day widens out.
Church Circle.
Dean, from junction of West and Church Circle to corner of Dean and Cathedral to-day.
Doctor, same as Franklin east of Cathedral.
Duke of Gloucester, from Market St. eastward; for name see p. 3.
East.
Francis, probably named for Gov. Francis Nicholson.
Goodwill, Conduit St. from Main to Duke of Gloucester.
Hanover, from Maryland Ave. southward.
King George's, now King George from College Ave. southward.
Market, ended at a marketplace laid out where the present junction is with Duke of Gloucester.
North.
Northeast, the present Maryland Ave.
Northwest.
Prince George, usually then called Prince George's.
Public Circle, present State Circle.
School.
Shipwright.
Sobieski, toward Murray Hill from junction of West and Calvert and at same angle to West as Calvert; named for the Polish hero Sobieski (d. 1696).
South, extended from present junction with Church Circle to corner of Charles and Cathedral.
Southeast, present Duke of Gloucester from Church Circle to Market St.
Tabernacle, present College Ave.
Temple, parallel to Franklin from Church Circle to Cathedral and half way to South St.
West.
Susquehannocks, 24.

T

Tasker, Ann (b. 1728), 96.
———, Benjamin (1690-1728), 95-6.
  Tomb in St. Anne's.
———, Benjamin, Jr. (d. 1760 in 39th year); tomb in St. Anne's.
———, Rebecca (b. 1724); married Daniel Dulany, Younger.
Taverns, 134, 135, 195, 198, 214.
  The following are most of the taverns which are mentioned in the *Maryland Gazette*, or about which we have any information:
  Coffee House, Main St. opposite Chancery Lane, see pages 134, 194-5, 198.
  Indian King, Main St., kept by Mr. McHard in 1782 and later by George Mann; Masons met here in 1749.
  Faris's, mentioned in 1775.
  Garretson's, mentioned in 1775.
  Hunter's, opposite McCloud's on West St.
  Johnson's, The Widow, mentioned in 1775.
  Mann's, see pages 134, 214; south corner of Main and Conduit Sts.
  McCloud's, No. 26 West St. Still standing.
  McHard's, mentioned in 1775.
  Middleton's, north corner of Market Space and Randall Sts.; still standing; kept by Mrs. Middleton and where Tuesday Club met several times; in 1771 meeting place of Jockey Club.
  Reynolds's, built 1737; corner of Church Circle and Franklin St.; still standing; sold by William Reynolds to Samuel Chase about 1771.
  Ship Tavern, on Duke of Gloucester (Southeast) St.; its proprietor, the Widow Marriott, died in 1755.
  Three Blue Balls, kept by John Ball, mentioned in 1755; northwest corner of Main and Conduit Sts.; house still on this site seems to have been an annex to the tavern, which was farther up street; once owned by John Hyde.
  Workman's, probably 10 Francis St.; still standing; in 1702, William Workman secured permission to build a house for a tavern on the school land, the house to revert to the school at his death.
Taylor, Adm. Henry C. (1842-1904), 259.
  Midn. N. A., 1860-3; instr., 1867-70, 1871-3.
Thackeray, W. M., 209.

Index 321

Theater, 71-81, 187, 194-9; Hallam company, 72-3; brick theater, 76-7; closed, 79; Miss Hallam, 80-2; Eddis's opinion, 81-2; used for church, 231.
Thompson, Col. Robert M. (1849——), 288.
    Midn. N. A., 1864-8; resigned from Navy in 1871.
Tilghman, James, 127.
——, Matthew (1718-1790), 162.
——, Capt. Samuel, 20.
Tilghman, Tench (1744-1786), 219.
Tilton, James, 218.
Tilton House, see "Houses."
Tobacco, 24, 50, 225.
Toleration Act, 11, 35.
Tories, 92-108, 185, 210-2, 226, 233.
Town Neck, 23.
Townshend Acts, 142.
Treasury Building, 31-2, 48, 59.
Tred Avon, 23.
Trenton, 216.
Trumbull, Jonathan, 215.
Tuesday Club, see "Clubs."

U

United States Navy, 7.
Unknown Soldier, 181.
Upper Marlborough, 73, 192, 195, 198, Appendix I.
Uriu, Rear Adm. Sotokichi (1857——), 281.
    Midn. N. A., 1877-81.
Utie, Nathaniel, 24.

V

Virginia, 12-3, 165.
Virginia Gazette, 72, 208.
Von Steuben, General, 177.

W

Waddell, James I. (1824-1886), instr. N. A., 1858-9; joined Confederates and commanded *Shenandoah* in cruise against Northern whalers in Pacific; built house on Prince George St., and resided there after Civil War.
War of 1812, 7.
Ward, Lieut. James H. (1806-1861), 250.
    Instr. N. A., 1845-7.

Warden, David B. (d. 1845), 241-4.
Washington Chair, said to have been used by Washington at resignation, now in possession of Pres. E. B. Garey, of St. John's College.
Washington College, 235.
Washington, George, 9, 66, 91, 102, 104, 107, 112, 129, 133-4, 163, 189-224; diaries, 194-198; expenses, 195-199; education of John Parke Custis, 201-8; opinions of Boucher and Eddis, 211-12; resignation, 214-233; education of G. W. P. Custis, 238-41.
———, Mrs. Martha, 202, 216.
Water; company incorporated in 1864.
Webster, Daniel, made address in Annapolis in 1851 at dinner to Constitutional Convention then in session.
Webster, Noah, lexicographer, see his Diary for Dec. 31, 1785, for his visit to Annapolis, description of town, and his lectures in the State House.
Weems, Mason Locks (1759-1825), born in Anne Arundel County, rector of All Hallows and Westminster Parishes, biographer of Washington; in 1814 preached in St. Anne's at meeting of Federalists celebrating the defeat of Napoleon; on march from Assembly Rooms after dinner the party was stoned by French sympathizers.
Welles, Gideon, 264.
Welsh names, 22-3.
West, Stephen, see Appendix I.
Whitefield, Rev. George, 232.
Whitehall, 107, 192.
Wildes, Capt. Frank (1843-1903), 259.
  Midn. N. A., 1860-3.
Wilkinson, William W., 258.
  Midn. N. A., 1859-61; appointed from S. C.
William of Orange, 27-8, 30, 37.
Williams & Co., 148-50.
Williams, James, 150-1.
———, Joseph, 150-1.
———, Thomas C., 153.
Williamsburg, 72, 74.
William and Mary, College of, 72.
Williamson, Hugh, 218.
Wilson, Woodrow, 99n.
Winans, Ross, 274.
Windmill Point, 152, 177, 247.

Worden, Commodore John L., 278.
  Supt. N. A., 1869-74.
Workmen's, see "Taverns."
Wormeley, Mr., 194-5.
Wren, Sir Christopher, see Foreword.
Wroth, L. C., 71n., 83n.
Wye, 23.
Wyoming, steam sloop stationed at N. A., 1888-9.

www.ingramcontent.com/pod-product-compliance
Lightning Source LLC
Chambersburg PA
CBHW071952220426
43662CB00009B/1099